# CISSP Exam Prep

## 550+ Practice Questions

### 2nd Edition

**www.versatileread.com**

# Document Control

| | | |
|---|---|---|
| Proposal Name | : | CISSP Exam Prep: 550+ Practice Questions |
| Document Edition | : | 2nd |
| Document Release Date | : | 13th July 2024 |
| Reference | : | CISSP |
| VR Product Code | : | 2024090202CISSP |

**Feedback:**

If you have any comments regarding the quality of this book or otherwise alter it to better suit your needs, you can contact us through email at info@versatileread.com

Please make sure to include the book's title and ISBN in your message.

# About the Contributors:

## Nouman Ahmed Khan

AWS/Azure/GCP-Architect, CCDE, CCIEx5 (R&S, SP, Security, DC, Wireless), CISSP, CISA, CISM, CRISC, ISO27K-LA is a Solution Architect working with a global telecommunication provider. He works with enterprises, mega-projects, and service providers to help them select the best-fit technology solutions. He also works as a consultant to understand customer business processes and helps select an appropriate technology strategy to support business goals. He has more than eighteen years of experience working with global clients. One of his notable experiences was his tenure with a large managed security services provider, where he was responsible for managing the complete MSSP product portfolio. With his extensive knowledge and expertise in various areas of technology, including cloud computing, network infrastructure, security, and risk management, Nouman has become a trusted advisor for his clients.

## Abubakar Saeed

Abubakar Saeed is a trailblazer in the realm of technology and innovation. With a rich professional journey spanning over twenty-nine years, Abubakar has seamlessly blended his expertise in engineering with his passion for transformative leadership. Starting humbly at the grassroots level, he has significantly contributed to pioneering the Internet in Pakistan and beyond. Abubakar's multifaceted experience encompasses managing, consulting, designing, and implementing projects, showcasing his versatility as a leader.

His exceptional skills shine in leading businesses, where he champions innovation and transformation. Abubakar stands as a testament to the power of visionary leadership, heading operations, solutions design, and integration. His emphasis on adhering to project timelines and exceeding customer expectations has set him apart as a great leader. With an unwavering commitment to adopting technology for operational simplicity and enhanced efficiency, Abubakar Saeed continues to inspire and drive change in the industry.

**Dr. Fahad Abdali**

Dr. Fahad Abdali is an esteemed leader with an outstanding twenty-year track record in managing diverse businesses. With a stellar educational background, including a bachelor's degree from the prestigious NED University of Engineers & Technology and a Ph.D. from the University of Karachi, Dr. Abdali epitomizes academic excellence and continuous professional growth.

Dr. Abdali's leadership journey is marked by his unwavering commitment to innovation and his astute understanding of industry dynamics. His ability to navigate intricate challenges has driven growth and nurtured organizational triumph. Driven by a passion for excellence, he stands as a beacon of inspiration within the business realm. With his remarkable leadership skills, Dr. Fahad Abdali continues to steer businesses toward unprecedented success, making him a true embodiment of a great leader.

**Muniza Kamran**

Muniza Kamran is a technical content developer in a professional field. She crafts clear and informative content that simplifies complex technical concepts for diverse audiences, with a passion for technology. Her expertise lies in Microsoft, cybersecurity, cloud security and emerging technologies, making her a valuable asset in the tech industry. Her dedication to quality and accuracy ensures that her writing empowers readers with valuable insights and knowledge. She has done certification in SQL database, database design, cloud solution architecture and NDG Linux unhatched from CISCO.

# Table of Contents

# About CISSP Certification

## Introduction

In today's digital age, where cyber threats are widespread, the demand for skilled information security professionals has never been higher. Among the many certifications available, the Certified Information Systems Security Professional (CISSP) stands out as a symbol of expertise and proficiency in cybersecurity. This section aims to guide you through the process of obtaining CISSP certification, offering valuable insights and practical tips to help you attain this esteemed credential.

## What is a CISSP?

CISSP stands for Certified Information Systems Security Professional. It is a globally recognized certification offered by the International System Security Certification Consortium, also known as (ISC)². CISSP is widely regarded as one of the most esteemed certifications in the fields of information security and cybersecurity. Individuals pursue CISSP certification to meet the demand for experienced and highly capable IT professionals who can effectively oversee an enterprise's cybersecurity by applying IT security-related concepts and theories. Upon successfully passing the certification exam, which typically lasts about six hours, CISSPs can assume various job roles, including Security Manager, Security Analyst, and Chief Information Security Officer. CISSPs prioritize maintaining a robust IT security system regardless of the job title.

# Certified Information Systems Security Professional Exam Format

The CISSP exam lasts for four hours and consists of multiple-choice and advanced creative questions, which will be discussed in more detail later. A score of 700 out of 1000 is required to pass the CISSP exam.

## CISSP-Certified Information Systems Security Professional

| | |
|---|---|
| **Prior Certification** <br> **Not Required** | **Exam Validity** <br> **3 Years** |
| **Exam Fee** <br> **$599 USD** | **Exam Duration** <br> **240 Minutes** |
| **No. of Questions** <br> **125-175 Questions** | **Passing Marks** <br> **700 out of 1000** |

**Recommended Experience**
**Minimum of five years of work experience in the domains of the CISSP CBK. Additional credential from the (ISC)[2] approved list. Education credit will only satisfy one year of experience.**

**Exam Format**
**Multiple Choice and advanced innovative items**

**Languages**
**English**

# How Much Do CISSP Holders Earn?

CISSPs are relatively rare in the industry, so those who pass the certification exam and meet the requirements are typically well-paid.

According to various sources, the average salary for a CISSP certified professional can vary depending on factors such as experience, location, and specific job title. Here's a breakdown from a few reputable sources:

- ZipRecruiter: Reports an average annual salary of $112,302 in the United States (as of March 15, 2024). They also provide a salary range from $21,000 to $165,000, with the 25th percentile at $95,500 and the 75th percentile at $128,000.
- Destination Certification: Offers average salary ranges based on job titles. For example, Chief Information Security Officers (CISOs) with CISSP certification can earn an average of $173,726, while Information Security Analysts might earn an average of $76,979.
- Simplilearn: States an average annual salary of $116,573 globally, indicating that CISSP certification is among the top-paying IT certifications.

Overall, CISSP certification can significantly boost your earning potential in the cybersecurity field. While exact salaries vary based on factors like experience and location, CISSPs can expect to earn anywhere from $75,000 to over $170,000 annually.

On the contrary, according to the Certification Magazine-Salary Survey 75 report, average salaries are as follows:

| Region | Average Salary (in U.S. Dollars) |
|---|---|
| Globally | $123,490 |
| United States | $135,510 |

The average global salaries reported by (ISC)² and CertMag differ due to variations in methodology. CertMag's figures encompass both U.S. and non-U.S. salaries, while (ISC)²'s statistics are derived from a broader industry-wide study, potentially offering a more representative view of actual averages. CertMag's data is based on a smaller sample size of only 55 respondents, whereas (ISC)²'s data likely involves a larger and more diverse sample.

## What Experience is Required to Become a CISSP?

Despite the growing demand for CISSPs, (ISC)² imposes stringent qualifications to ensure that only highly capable and experienced professionals earn the title. While the industry offers lucrative opportunities, the requirements for CISSPs are comprehensive.

Firstly, CISSP applicants must possess at least five years of relevant working experience in IT security. This experience must align with the eight domains of the (ISC)² CISSP CBK:

1. Security and Risk Management
2. Asset Security
3. Security Architecture and Engineering
4. Communication and Network Security
5. Identity and Access Management (IAM)
6. Security Assessment and Testing
7. Security Operations
8. Software Development Security

Moreover, to meet the requirements of these domains, the (ISC)² mandates experience in any of the following positions:

- Chief Information Security Officer
- Chief Information Officer
- Director of Security
- IT Director/Manager
- Security Systems Engineer
- Security Analyst
- Security Manager
- Security Auditor
- Security Architect
- Security Consultant
- Network Architect

## Job Opportunities with CISSP Certifications

Roles of CISSP-Certified Professionals:

## Information Security Analyst

In the role of an Information Security Analyst, individuals with CISSP certification play a critical role in strengthening an organization's digital infrastructure and systems. They are responsible for analyzing and implementing robust security measures to proactively defend against a wide range of cyber threats, ensuring the resilience of the organization's information assets.

## Security Consultant

CISSP-certified professionals serve as adept Security Consultants, offering specialized guidance in crafting and implementing security protocols. Their role involves meticulous examination of existing security frameworks, providing strategic insights, and implementing tailored solutions to fortify against evolving cyber threats and vulnerabilities. They assess clients' specific security needs, ensuring robust protection against potential risks.

## Chief Information Security Officer (CISO)

As Chief Information Security Officers, CISSP-certified experts lead and manage an organization's comprehensive security program. They formulate and execute strategies to safeguard information assets, ensuring the highest standards of cybersecurity.

## Security Software Developer

CISSP professionals in this role focus on developing secure software and applications. Their expertise ensures that the software development process integrates robust security measures, protecting against vulnerabilities and potential breaches.

## Risk Manager

CISSP-certified Risk Managers identify and mitigate potential security risks within an organization. They conduct thorough risk assessments, develop mitigation strategies, and implement measures to minimize the impact of security threats.

These roles highlight the versatility and importance of CISSP certification across various domains. They underscore the crucial role CISSP professionals play in maintaining a secure and resilient digital landscape.

# Benefits of CISSP Certification

- Demonstrates working knowledge of information security.
- Provides a career differentiator, enhancing credibility and marketability.
- Grants access to valuable resources such as peer networking and idea exchange.
- Offers access to a network of global industry experts and subject matter/domain experts.
- Facilitates access to broad-based security information resources.
- Provides a business and technology orientation to risk management.

# Alternative Paths to Achieving CISSP Certification

Not everyone meets the strict CISSP certification requirements. However, there are alternative paths to enter the industry:

1. **Become an (ISC)² Associate:** By working as an (ISC)² Associate, individuals can fast-track their cybersecurity career despite lacking the requisite experience. This role provides opportunities for learning and growth within the industry.

2. **Obtain CompTIA Certifications:** CompTIA certifications, such as A+, Security+, and Network+, can help kickstart a cybersecurity career by bolstering credentials and demonstrating specific skills and knowledge.

3. **Pursue SSCP Certification:** Another option for meeting CISSP requirements is to earn the Systems Security Certified Professional (SSCP) credential from (ISC)². This certification serves as a stepping stone toward CISSP certification while providing comprehensive preparation and understanding of the field.

# Demand of CISSP Certification in 2024

The demand for CISSP certification is expected to remain strong in 2024 for several reasons:

- **Growing Cybersecurity Threats:** As cybercrime continues to rise, organizations are increasingly looking for qualified professionals to protect their data and systems. The CISSP certification validates a candidate's understanding of cybersecurity best practices and makes them more competitive in the job market.
- **Global Recognition:** CISSP is a vendor-neutral certification that is recognized worldwide. This makes it a valuable asset for professionals who want to work in any industry or location.
- **Focus on Security Management:** CISSP goes beyond technical skills and emphasizes security management principles. This makes CISSP holders well-suited for leadership roles in cybersecurity.

## Practice Questions

1. Which of the following describes the principle of least privilege in information security?

A. Users should be granted the minimum permissions necessary to perform their jobs.

B. All users should have administrative access to simplify troubleshooting

C. Security permissions should be increased as users gain experience

D. Users should only have access to information relevant to their current tasks.

2. Which of the following is NOT a domain covered in the CISSP Common Body of Knowledge (CBK)?

A. Business Continuity and Disaster Recovery (BCDR)

B. Asset security

C. Software development security

D. Security and risk management

3. Which type of security control aims to prevent unauthorized access to a system?

A. Preventive

B. Detective

C. Corrective

D. Risk

4. What type of attack is most likely indicated when a hacker gains access to a user's account without authorization?

A. Social engineering

B. Password spraying

C. Phishing

D. Man-in-the-Middle (MitM) attack

5. Which of the following is the BEST practice for password management?

A. Using the same password for all accounts

B. Sharing passwords with colleagues

C. Using strong and unique passwords for each account

D. Writing passwords down on a sticky note

6. Which security assessment method involves simulating an attack to identify vulnerabilities?

A. Vulnerability scanning

B. Penetration testing

C. Risk assessment

D. Security audit

7. Which type of encryption scrambles data during transmission but allows authorized users to decrypt it?

A. Symmetric Encryption

B. Asymmetric Encryption

C. Hashing

D. Steganography

8. What is the purpose of a Security Information and Event Management (SIEM) system?

A. To block unauthorized access attempts

B. To collect and analyze security logs from various sources

C. To encrypt data at rest

D. To provide secure remote access

9. Which of the following is a common type of social engineering attack?

A. Phishing

B. Denial-of-Service (DoS) attack

C. SQL injection

D. Zero-day attack

10. What is the CIA triad in information security?

A. Confidentiality, Integrity, and Authentication

B. Confidentiality, Integrity, and Availability

C. Confidentiality, Impact, and Availability

D. Confidentiality, Intrusion Detection, and Access Control

11. What is the primary goal of risk management in information security?

A. Total elimination of all risks

B. Minimizing risk to an acceptable level

C. Ignoring risks

D. Transferring all risks to a third-party

12. In the context of information security, what does the term "data classification" refer to?

A. Sorting data alphabetically

B. Categorizing data based on its sensitivity and criticality

C. Encrypting all data

D. Backing up data regularly

13. What is the purpose of a firewall in network security?

A. Encrypting data transmission

B. Monitoring and controlling incoming and outgoing network traffic

C. Blocking all network traffic

D. Managing user authentication

14. Which of the following protocols is commonly used for securing email communications?

A. HTTP

B. FTP

C. SMTP

D. SNMP

15. Which category of control is designed to give legitimate users a sense of ownership of the space while signaling to potential offenders that their presence is noticeable?

A. Natural access control
   B. Natural surveillance
   C. Natural territorial reinforcement
   D. Mechanical access control

16. What is the main goal of penetration testing?

A. Identifying vulnerabilities in a system

B. Installing security patches

C. Encrypting data at rest

D. Monitoring network traffic

17. What is the purpose of an incident response plan?

A. Preventing all incidents from occurring

B. Minimizing the impact of security incidents

C. Ignoring security incidents

D. Reporting all incidents to the media

18. What is the primary goal of incorporating security into the Software Development Life Cycle (SDLC)?

A. Reducing software development time

B. Enhancing user experience

C. Identifying and mitigating security issues early in the development process

D. Ignoring security concerns until after deployment

19. What is the purpose of a security policy in an organization?

A. Providing guidelines for employee dress code

B. Defining the organization's approach to managing security

C. Monitoring employee productivity

D. Managing financial transactions

20. What is the primary focus of physical security controls?

A. Protecting digital data

B. Safeguarding against environmental hazards

C. Implementing access controls

D. Encrypting communication channels

21. Which of the following is an implication of the principle of Separation of Duties (SoD) in information security?

A. Users should be granted all necessary permissions to avoid bottlenecks.

B. Critical tasks should be divided among multiple individuals to reduce the risk of fraud.

C. Administrative privileges should be routinely rotated among users.

D. Access to sensitive data should be restricted based on job roles and responsibilities.

22. A DMZ (Demilitarized Zone) is a network segment that separates the internal network from the public internet. What is the primary purpose of a DMZ?

A. To encrypt all traffic entering and leaving the internal network.

B. To provide a controlled area for hosting public-facing services.

C. To isolate and quarantine infected devices.

D. To segment the internal network for improved performance.

23. Which of the following is a type of cryptography that uses a single key for both encryption and decryption?

A. Asymmetric encryption

B. Symmetric encryption

C. Hashing

D. Steganography

24. Which security standard specifies requirements for a formal Information Security Management System (ISMS)?

A. NIST SP 800-53

B. Payment Card Industry Data Security Standard (PCI DSS)

C. Health Insurance Portability and Accountability Act (HIPAA)

D. ISO 27001

25. Which type of security testing involves scanning a system for known vulnerabilities?

A. Penetration testing

B. Vulnerability scanning

C. Risk assessment

D. Security audit

26. What is the main reason for conducting a risk analysis in the site planning process for facility security?
    A. To comply with industry best practices
    B. To identify the organization's vulnerabilities, threats, and business impacts
    C. To ensure employee productivity
    D. To reduce insurance premiums

27. Which of the following is a key benefit of using Multi-Factor Authentication (MFA)?

A. It eliminates the need for strong passwords.

B. It strengthens authentication by requiring additional verification factors beyond a password.

C. It automatically detects and blocks phishing attacks.

D. It simplifies the login process for users.

28. Which of the following is a disadvantage of using cloud-based storage services?

A. Decreased scalability and flexibility.

B. Potential loss of control over data security.

C. Reduced hardware and maintenance costs.

D. None of the above.

29. What does the acronym BCP refer to?

A. Business Continuity and Penetration Testing

B. Business Continuity and Planning

C. Business Critical Processes

D. Breach Control Protocol

30. Which of the following is NOT a common type of Denial-of-Service (DoS) attack?

A. Smurf attack

B. Ping Flood attack

C. Man-in-the-Middle (MitM) attack

D. SYN Flood attack

31. What is the primary goal of information security governance?

A. To implement technical controls

B. To ensure compliance with regulations

C. To protect information assets and support business objectives

D. To detect and respond to security incidents

32. In what type of area should smoke detectors be installed for effective fire detection in a facility?
A. Only in office areas

B. Above suspended ceilings and below-raised floors

C. Exclusively in restrooms

D. Solely in server rooms

33. What is the primary goal of security architecture?

A. To design secure systems and architectures

B. To implement security policies

C. To conduct vulnerability assessments

D. To train employees on security best practices

34. Which of the following is a common security control for securing wireless networks?

A. Firewall

B. Intrusion Detection System (IDS)

C. Virtual Private Network (VPN)

D. Wi-Fi Protected Access 3 (WPA3)

35. What is the primary goal of Crime Prevention Through Environmental Design (CPTED)?

A. To harden targets using physical and artificial barriers

B. To reduce crime by directly affecting human behavior through environmental design

C. To implement high-tech security systems

D. To provide aesthetically pleasing landscapes

36. What is the primary goal of a vulnerability assessment?

A. To exploit vulnerabilities in a system

B. To identify and quantify vulnerabilities in a system

C. To design secure systems

D. To create security policies

37. What type of fire suppression system should ideally be used in data processing environments to avoid unnecessary water damage?

A. Wet pipe system
B. Dry pipe system
C. Pre-action system
D. Deluge system

38. During a security audit, what is the primary objective of verifying the effectiveness of security controls?

A. Identifying vulnerabilities

B. Assessing compliance with policies

C. Ensuring confidentiality of data

D. Simulating real-world attack scenarios

39. What is the purpose of a Business Impact Analysis (BIA)?

A. Evaluating the financial impact of security incidents

B. Assessing the impact of security policies on business operations

C. Identifying critical business processes and their dependencies

D. Measuring the effectiveness of security controls

40. What is the primary purpose of a Hardware Security Module (HSM)?

A. Securing network communications

B. Encrypting stored data

C. Authenticating users

D. Protecting cryptographic keys

41. Which of the following is the MOST important concept in secure software development according to the CISSP?

A. Extensive code reviews after development are sufficient.

B. Security should be integrated throughout the entire software development lifecycle (SDLC).

C. Developers should prioritize speed and functionality over security features.

D. Open-source software inherently poses a higher security risk.

42. A user reports receiving a suspicious email claiming to be from their bank. The email asks them to click a link to verify their account information. What type of social engineering attack is this most likely an example of?

A. Quid pro quo

B. Phishing

C. Pretexting

D. Watering Hole

43. Which of the following is a primary function of a Security Operations Center (SOC)?

A. Conducting security audits and penetration testing.

B. Monitoring and analyzing security events for threats and incidents.

C. Implementing and managing security controls on devices.

D. Providing user education and security awareness training.

44. What does the acronym refer to?

A. Public Infrastructure Information

B. Protected Internal Information

C. Personally Identifiable Information

D. Proprietary Intellectual Information

45. Which type of security control aims to detect and report security incidents?

A. Preventive

B. Detective

C. Corrective

D. Risk

46. Which of the following is a benefit of using encryption at rest?

A. It protects data during transmission across networks.

B. It ensures the integrity of data by preventing unauthorized modification.

C. It renders data unusable if the storage device is stolen or lost.

D. It simplifies data access for authorized users.

47. What is the difference between a vulnerability and a threat in the context of information security?

A. A vulnerability is an exploit, while a threat is a capability to exploit it.

B. A threat is an attacker's motivation, while a vulnerability is a weakness in a system.

C. There is no difference; they are interchangeable terms.

D. A vulnerability is a security control, and a threat is a security incident.

48. Which of the following best practices is recommended for creating strong passwords?

A. Using short and easy-to-remember passwords.

B. Including personal information like birthdays or pet names.

C. Using a combination of uppercase and lowercase letters, numbers, and symbols.

D. Reusing the same password for multiple accounts.


49. What does the concept of "defense in depth" represent in information security?

A. Relying on a single security control to protect against all threats.

B. Implementing multiple layers of security controls to mitigate risks.

C. Focusing security efforts solely on perimeter defenses.

D. Prioritizing detection and response capabilities over preventive controls.


50. What is the purpose of implementing mantraps in a secure facility?
    A. To provide a rest area for employees
    B. To detect fire or smoke within the facility
    C. To prevent piggybacking and control access to secure areas
    D. To serve as an emergency exit for personnel


51. What is the primary role of a Chief Information Security Officer (CISO) in an organization?

A. Implementing technical controls

B. Ensuring compliance with regulations

C. Managing day-to-day IT operations

D. Overseeing the organization's information security program

52. What is the purpose of an Information Asset Inventory?

A. Identifying physical assets

B. Categorizing and managing information assets

C. Creating financial reports for stakeholders

D. Monitoring network traffic

53. Which security model focuses on data confidentiality, integrity, and availability?

A. Biba

B. Bell-LaPadula

C. Clark-Wilson

D. Brewer-Nash

54. What is the primary purpose of a Virtual Private Network (VPN)?

A. Monitoring network traffic

B. Encrypting communication over untrusted networks

C. Filtering malicious emails

D. Securing physical access to network devices

55. What should security professionals think about when considering physical security?

A. Only the use of guards and fences

B. The potential for technology-oriented security breaches

C. The ways individuals can physically enter an environment and cause damage

D. Protecting computer cases means keeping them safe from damage or harm.

56. Which of the following is an example of a supply system threat?
A. Vandalism
B. Power distribution outages
C. Unauthorized access
D. Strikes

57. What should a good security plan consider regarding threats?

A. Only manufactured threats
B. Only natural environmental threats
C. Only supply system threats
D. A variety of threats, including natural, supply system, manufactured, and politically motivated threats

58. What is one of the goals of good security in an organization?
 A. To make employees feel restricted
 B. To prevent employees from focusing on their tasks
 C. To encourage attackers by presenting a challenge
 D. To provide a secure and predictable environment

59. What is the purpose of a Privacy Impact Assessment (PIA)?

A. Assessing the impact of security policies on business operations

B. Evaluating the financial impact of security incidents

C. Identifying and assessing the privacy risks of a project or system

D. Creating disaster recovery plans

60. In the context of cryptography, what does the term "key escrow" refer to?

A. Storing cryptographic keys in a secure vault

B. Distributing cryptographic keys to multiple parties

C. Backing up cryptographic keys with a trusted third-party

D. Encrypting communication channels

61. Which of the following is the MOST important consideration for secure password hashing according to the CISSP?

A. Using a simple hashing algorithm like MD5.

B. Storing password hashes in plain text.

C. Employing a strong, one-way hashing algorithm with a salt.

D. Allowing users to choose weak passwords for ease of use.

62. You suspect your organization's website may be vulnerable to a SQL injection attack. What type of security control can help mitigate this risk?

A. Data encryption at rest

B. Input validation and sanitization

C. Firewalls with deep packet inspection

D. Regular vulnerability scanning

63. Which of the following is NOT a manufactured threat to an organization's security?
A. Employee errors and accidents
B. Unauthorized access
C. Natural disasters
D. Vandalism

64. What is the primary purpose of using a digital certificate in secure communication?

A. To encrypt data transmission.

B. To authenticate the identity of communicating parties.

C. To ensure data integrity during transmission.

D. To compress data for faster transmission.

65. How does the balance life safety concerns with other security measures?
 A. By installing more advanced technology
 B. By allowing unrestricted access
 C. By implementing a layered defense model
 D. By barring all doors permanently

66. Which of the following describes a Business Continuity and Disaster recovery (BCDR) best practice?

A. Backing up data only on weekends to minimize storage requirements.

B. Regularly testing the BCDR plan to ensure its effectiveness.

C. Storing all backups in the same physical location as the primary data.

D. Relying solely on cloud-based backups without local copies.

67. What is the primary consideration in all aspects of site and facility security?
 A. Protecting the computing systems
 B. Ensuring the confidentiality of data
 C. Protecting human life
 D. Preventing unauthorized access

68. Which of the following is a type of malware that replicates itself and spreads to other devices?

A. Logic bomb

B. Worm

C. Rootkit

D. Trojan horse

69. Which of the following is the PRIMARY objective of a Security Assessment and Authorization (SA&A) process according to CISSP?

A. To identify and patch all vulnerabilities in a system.

B. To document existing security controls and assess their effectiveness.

C. To continuously monitor the security posture of an organization.

D. To provide security awareness training to all employees.

70. A user clicks on a malicious link in a phishing email and infects their computer with malware. What type of control would have MOST likely helped prevent this incident?

A. Web filtering to block access to malicious websites.

B. Data encryption at rest.

C. Regular vulnerability scanning of user devices.

D. Multi-factor Authentication (MFA).

71. Which of the following statements is TRUE about network segmentation in information security?

A. It is not a recommended security practice in modern networks.

B. It involves dividing the network into smaller, isolated segments to limit the blast radius of security incidents.

C. All network traffic should be allowed to flow freely between all segments.

D. Segmentation is only necessary for highly sensitive data.

72. You are implementing a new cloud-based application for your organization. Which security control should be a TOP priority to consider?

A. Data encryption in transit

B. User access controls and permissions

C. Firewall configuration for the cloud environment

D. Data Loss Prevention (DLP) for cloud storage

73. What type of attack exploits the algebraic structures within an encryption algorithm?
 A. Side-Channel attack
 B. Algebraic attack
 C. Social engineering attack
 D. Differential cryptanalysis

74. Which cryptographic algorithm is considered quantum-resistant and is recommended for securing data against future quantum computing threats?

A. AES-256

B. RSA-4096

C. ECC (Elliptic Curve Cryptography)

D. Post-Quantum Cryptography (PQC)

75. Which of the following best practices is recommended for secure Mobile Device Management (MDM)?

A. Allowing users to install any application they desire on company-owned devices.

B. Enforcing strong password policies and remote wipe capabilities for lost or stolen devices.

C. Disabling encryption on mobile devices for improved performance.

D. Providing users with administrative privileges on their work phones.

76. What are two countermeasures against replay attacks?
A. Differential cryptanalysis and linear cryptanalysis
B. Timestamps and sequence numbers
C. Chosen-plaintext and chosen-ciphertext attacks
D. Algebraic and analytic attacks

77. You suspect a Denial-of-Service (DoS) attack is targeting your web server. What is the MOST important action to take during this incident?

A. Identify and block the source of the attack traffic.

B. Shut down the web server completely to prevent further attacks.

C. Analyze the attack pattern and implement mitigation strategies.

D. Change all user passwords as a precaution.

78. What is the primary purpose of a risk assessment in information security?

A. To eliminate all risks

B. To transfer all risks to a third-party

C. To identify and prioritize risks to make informed decisions

D. To implement technical controls

79. What is the purpose of side-channel attacks in cryptography?
A. To directly break the encryption algorithm using mathematical tools.
B. To modify the encryption system files.
C. To gain information about the encryption key by observing external information.
D. To perform brute-force attacks by trying every possible key.

80. What is the primary purpose of a stateful firewall?

A. To filter traffic based on IP addresses

B. To inspect and track the state of active connections

C. To encrypt all network traffic

D. To block specific websites

81. What is the role of a RADIUS server in IAM?

A. Providing secure file storage

B. Authenticating and authorizing remote users

C. Encrypting data transmission

D. Managing access control lists

82. What is the primary goal of a security audit?

A. Identifying vulnerabilities in a system

B. Assessing the effectiveness of security controls and policies

C. Encrypting sensitive data

D. Conducting penetration testing

83. What is the main difference between public and secret algorithms in cryptography?
A. Public algorithms are weaker than secret algorithms.
B. The NSA does not use secret algorithms.
C. Public algorithms are released for peer review, while secret algorithms are not.
D. Secret algorithms are developed by a larger team of cryptographers.

84. What is the primary goal of input validation in secure coding practices?

A. Enhancing user experience

B. Reducing software development time

C. Preventing injection attacks and improving security

D. Ignoring user input altogether

85. What is the primary purpose of a Business Continuity Plan (BCP)?

A. Preventing all business disruptions

B. Identifying and responding to security incidents

C. Ensuring the availability of critical business functions during disruptions

D. Ignoring business disruptions altogether

86. What was differential cryptanalysis primarily used against successfully?
A. RSA encryption
B. Block algorithms like DES
C. Known-plaintext attacks
D. Social engineering attacks

87. Which of the following is the MOST important concept in disaster recovery according to the CISSP?

A. Implementing complex technical controls to prevent disasters entirely.

B. Regularly testing and updating the disaster recovery plan to ensure effectiveness.

C. Focusing solely on recovering critical business functions after a disaster.

D. Stockpiling large amounts of supplies in anticipation of potential disasters.

88. A user reports receiving a USB drive containing a suspicious executable file. What is the BEST course of action to advise the user?

A. Open the file to see what it does.

B. Plug the USB drive into a work computer and scan the file with antivirus software.

C. Do not open the file and delete the USB drive securely.

D. Forward the file to the IT department for analysis.

89. Which of the following best describes the concept of steganography in information security?

A. Encrypting data to render it unreadable.

B. Hiding data within another file.

C. Using digital signatures to ensure data integrity.

D. Employing access controls to restrict data access.

90. Which security standard focuses on the secure handling of credit card information?

A. Health Insurance Portability and Accountability Act (HIPAA)

B. Payment Card Industry Data Security Standard (PCI DSS)

C. General Data Protection Regulation (GDPR )

D. Federal Information Security Management Act (FISMA)

91. What is the primary purpose of using a honeypot in a security context?

A. To encrypt data at rest and in transit.

B. To attract and deceive attackers to learn about their tactics.

C. To provide a sandbox environment for testing security tools.

D. To centrally manage and update security controls across devices.

92. Which of the following statements is TRUE about multi-factor authentication (MFA)?

A. MFA eliminates the need for strong passwords.

B. MFA requires two or more verification factors beyond just a password for user authentication.

C. MFA is only necessary for high-privileged user accounts.

D. Fingerprint scanners are not a valid form of MFA.

93. A company implements a new security policy that restricts employee access to social media websites during work hours. What type of security control is this?

A. Preventive

B. Detective

C. Corrective

D. Risk

94. Which of the following is a benefit of using a centralized logging system for security events?

A. It increases the complexity of security event management.

B. It simplifies log collection, analysis, and correlation for security investigations.

C. It requires additional hardware and software resources for each device.

D. It makes it more difficult to detect and respond to security incidents.

95. What does the concept of "availability" mean in the CIA triad of information security?

A. Ensuring data confidentiality and preventing unauthorized access.

B. Protecting data integrity and maintaining its accuracy and completeness.

C. Guaranteeing authorized users have timely and reliable access to data.

D. Implementing security controls to detect and respond to security incidents.

96. What is the difference between standard and adaptive chosen-ciphertext attacks?
A. Adaptive attacks can modify the next attack based on previous findings.
B. Standard attacks use brute-force methods, while adaptive attacks do not.
C. Adaptive attacks only use statistical analysis.
D. There is no difference; they are the same type of attack.

97. Your organization is implementing a new cloud-based storage solution. Which security principle should be a TOP priority to consider?

A. Data encryption at rest and in transit

B. Implementing firewalls on user devices

C. Disabling Data Loss Prevention (DLP) for cloud storage

D. Providing administrative access to all users for cloud storage

98. Which of the following best describes the concept of a Denial-of-Service (DoS) attack?

A. Gaining unauthorized access to a system to steal data.

B. Exploiting vulnerabilities in a system to install malware.

C. Overwhelming a system with traffic to render it unavailable to legitimate users.

D. Tricking users into revealing sensitive information through social engineering.

99. What is the goal of a chosen-ciphertext attack?
A. To choose and encrypt plaintext without knowing the key.
B. To alter the encryption algorithm.
C. To discover the key by selecting ciphertexts to be decrypted.
D. To intercept plaintext messages.

100. How does a chosen-plaintext attack differ from other types of attacks?
A. The attacker does not know the plaintext.
B. The attacker can choose the plaintext to be encrypted.
C. The attacker only has access to the ciphertext.
D. The attacker modifies the encryption algorithm.

101. What kind of attack involves the attacker having both the plaintext and corresponding ciphertext, and aims to find the encryption key?
A. Ciphertext-Only
B. Known-Plaintext
C. Chosen-Ciphertext
D. Meet-in-the-Middle

102. You suspect a user's computer may be infected with malware. What type of security control can help detect and potentially remove the malware?

A. Data Loss Prevention (DLP)

B. Endpoint Detection and Response (EDR)

C. Web Application Firewall (WAF)

D. Security Information and Event Management (SIEM)

103. Which type of attack involves an attacker gaining access to the ciphertext of several messages and attempting to discover the encryption key?
A. Known-Plaintext
B. Chosen-Plaintext
C. Ciphertext-Only
D. Chosen-Ciphertext

104. Which of the following is the MOST important consideration for secure communication according to CISSP?

A. Disabling encryption altogether for faster data transfer.

B. Implementing strong encryption protocols like AES or TLS to protect data confidentiality.

C. Relying solely on access controls to restrict unauthorized access.

D. Use the same password for all communication channels.

105. A user reports receiving a phone call from someone claiming to be from IT support, requesting remote access to their computer to fix a critical issue. What type of social engineering attack is this most likely an example of?

A. Phishing

B. Pretexting

C. Quid pro quo

D. Watering hole attack

106. Which of the following best describes the concept of network segmentation in information security?

A. Connecting all devices on a network to a single central switch.

B. Dividing the network into smaller, isolated segments to limit the blast radius of security incidents.

C. Disabling firewalls on all network devices.

D. Granting unrestricted network access to all users.

107. Your company is developing a new web application. Which security principle should be incorporated from the beginning of the development process?

A. Security testing should be conducted only after the application is developed.

B. Security should be integrated throughout the entire software Development Lifecycle (SDLC).

C. Focusing solely on perimeter security measures is sufficient.

D. Developers should prioritize speed and functionality over security features.

108. Which of the following is a use of Digital Rights Management (DRM)?

A. To recover corrupted cryptographic keys
B. To control access to copyrighted data
C. To store cryptographic keys in the TPM
D. To generate one-time passwords for authentication

109. Which of the following is NOT a recommended practice for key management?

A. Keys should be backed up or escrowed in case of emergencies.
B. Keys should be transmitted in cleartext for ease of use.
C. The key's lifetime should correspond with the sensitivity of the data it protects.
D. Keys should be properly destroyed when their lifetime ends.

110. What is the role of the Key Distribution Center (KDC) in cryptography?
A. To generate and distribute digital signatures
B. To store, distribute, and maintain cryptographic keys
C. To serve as the primary encryption mechanism for messages
D. To act as the sole recovery agent for lost keys

111. What does the concept of "integrity" mean in the CIA triad of information security?

A. Ensuring data confidentiality and preventing unauthorized access.

B. Guaranteeing authorized users have timely and reliable access to data.

C. Protecting data accuracy and completeness and preventing unauthorized modification.

D. Implementing security controls to detect and respond to security incidents.

112. What does the term 'non-repudiation' refer to in the context of cryptosystems?

A. The inability to decrypt a message without the appropriate key
B. The action of denying the sending of a message
C. The prevention of unauthorized access to a message
D. The assurance that the sender cannot deny sending the message

113. What is the primary goal of privacy by design in the context of information security?

A. Ensuring data availability

B. Integrating privacy measures into systems and processes from the beginning

C. Encrypting all sensitive data

D. Conducting regular security audits

114. What is the purpose of a threat modeling process in security architecture?

A. Identifying and prioritizing potential security threats

B. Developing secure coding practices

C. Encrypting communication channels

D. Implementing access controls

115. Which encryption protocol is commonly used to secure web traffic?

A. IPsec

B. SSL/TLS

C. PGP

D. SSH

116. What is the primary purpose of Single Sign-On (SSO) in IAM?

A. Simplifying user authentication by using multiple credentials

B. Allowing users to use the same set of credentials across multiple systems

C. Encrypting user passwords

D. Implementing multi-factor authentication

117. What is the primary purpose of a security baseline?

A. Assessing the effectiveness of security controls

B. Identifying and quantifying vulnerabilities in a system

C. Establishing a minimum level of security for systems and applications

D. Encrypting sensitive data

118. Which key is installed in the TPM during manufacturing and cannot be altered?

A. Storage Root Key (SRK)
B. Platform Configuration Registers (PCR)
C. Endorsement Key (EK)
D. Attestation Identity Key (AIK)

119. What is the primary purpose of secure coding guidelines?

A. Accelerating the software development process

B. Improving user experience

C. Identifying and mitigating security vulnerabilities in code

D. Ignoring security concerns until after deployment

120. What is the purpose of quantitative risk analysis?

A. Identifying and assessing risks based on subjective judgment

B. Evaluating risks using numerical values and metrics

C. Encrypting sensitive data

D. Creating disaster recovery plans

121. What is the primary goal of Data Loss Prevention (DLP) technology?

A. Encrypting data transmission

B. Preventing unauthorized access to data

C. Monitoring and controlling the movement of sensitive data

D. Conducting vulnerability assessments

122. Which of the following is NOT a function of the Trusted Platform Module (TPM)?
A. Binding a hard disk drive to a computing system
B. Sealing a system's configurations
C. Directly protecting a system against electromagnetic interference
D. Storing cryptographic keys and hashes

123. A user clicks on a malicious link in a spam email and downloads malware onto their computer. What type of control MOST likely failed to prevent this incident?

A. Data encryption in transit

B. User education and awareness training

C. Firewalls with deep packet inspection

D. Strong password policies

124. Which U.S. government standard is associated with digital signatures?

A. Digital Signature Algorithm (DSA)
B. Digital Signature Standard (DSS)
C. Secure Hash Algorithm (SHA)
D. Key Distribution Center (KDC)

125. You are implementing a new cloud-based service for your organization. Which security control should be a TOP priority to consider?

A. Data encryption at rest and in transit

B. Implementing firewalls on user devices

C. Disabling Multi-Factor Authentication (MFA) for cloud access

D. Granting administrative privileges to all cloud service users

126. What is the purpose of a digital signature?
A. To provide confidentiality by encrypting the message content
B. To confirm the identity of the sender and the integrity of the message
C. To authorize user access to network resources
D. To encrypt the entire message for secure transmission

127. What is a critical step in ensuring the effectiveness of a disaster recovery plan?

A. Performing a single backup of data.

B. Regularly testing the disaster recovery plan.

C. Keeping all backups on-site.

D. Creating the disaster recovery plan once and never revisiting it.

128. Which of the following best practices is recommended for secure password management?

A. Using short and easy-to-remember passwords.

B. Including personal information like birthdays or pet names in passwords.

C. Using a password manager to store complex, unique passwords for different accounts.

D. Reusing the same password for all personal and work accounts.

129. Which security service is NOT directly provided by a PKI?
A. Encryption
B. Virus scanning
C. Authentication
D. Non-repudiation

130. What is the primary goal of an Information Security Management System (ISMS) based on ISO 27001?

A. Ensuring system availability

B. Achieving regulatory compliance

C. Establishing a framework for information security governance

D. Encrypting all data

131. What does the term "data at rest" refer to in the context of information security?

A. Data in transit between systems

B. Data actively being processed by a computer system

C. Data stored on non-volatile storage devices

D. Data exchanged in communication channels

132. Which cryptographic algorithm is commonly used for secure email communication?

A. RSA

B. AES

C. SHA-256

D. Diffie-Hellman

133. Which entity or function is NOT part of a PKI?
A. Certificate repository
B. Email client
C. Key backup and recovery system
D. Timestamping

134. What is the primary goal of a Role-Based Access Control (RBAC) System?

A. Assigning permissions based on user attributes

B. Assigning permissions based on job roles

C. Encrypting user credentials

D. Implementing multi-factor authentication

135. How can cross-certification between independent PKIs be described?

A. It is a protocol to revoke certificates
B. It is the process of establishing a trust relationship between CAs
C. It is a backup system for digital certificates
D. It is a method of encrypting emails between users

136. What does the X.509 standard dictate in the context of PKI?
A. The protocols for secure email transmission
B. The process for cross-certification between CAs
C. The fields used in a digital certificate and their valid values
D. The encryption algorithms used for certificate encryption

137. What is the primary objective of code review in the software development process?

A. Accelerating the development process

B. Identifying and fixing security vulnerabilities in the code

C. Enhancing the user interface

D. Ignoring security concerns until after deployment

138. Which protocol is being used more often instead of the CRL for real-time validation of certificates?
A. SMTP
B. OCSP
C. PKI
D. X.509

139. What is a Certificate Revocation List (CRL)?
A. A list of all email servers in an organization
B. A list of all the revoked digital certificates
C. A protocol for real-time validation of certificates
D. A list of all registered certificates in the PKI

140. What is the role of a Registration Authority (RA) in a PKI?
A. To create and sign digital certificates
B. To maintain and revoke certificates
C. To verify individuals' identity and initiate the certification process
D. To supply the public keys to users

141. A user reports a suspicious website that appears to be a legitimate e-commerce site but might be a phishing attempt. What is the MOST appropriate action for the user to take?

A. Enter their login credentials on the website and see if it works.

B. Report the suspicious website to the IT security team.

C. Bookmark the website for future reference.

D. Click the "forgot password" link and reset their password for the legitimate website.

142. Which of the following best describes the concept of risk management in information security?

A. Eliminating all security risks.

B. Identifying, analyzing, prioritizing, and implementing controls to mitigate security risks.

C. Focusing solely on detecting and responding to security incidents.

D. Transferring all security risks to a third-party vendor.

143. Your company uses a cloud-based storage service. Which security control is MOST important to implement to protect data at rest?

A. Data Loss Prevention (DLP) to monitor data exfiltration attempts.

B. Strong access controls to restrict unauthorized access to cloud storage.

C. Data encryption is at rest within the cloud storage service.

D. Multi-factor authentication (MFA) for all user accounts.

144. Which organization or server is responsible for creating and signing digital certificates in a PKI?

A. Registration Authority (RA)
B. Certificate Repository
C. Certificate Authority (CA)
D. Key Backup and Recovery System

145. Which of the following statements is TRUE about incident response (IR)?

A. The primary goal of IR is to assign blame for the security incident.

B. A well-defined IR plan helps to contain, eradicate, and recover from security incidents effectively.

C. Organizations should not document their IR plan to avoid giving away sensitive information.

D. Security incidents should be ignored if they do not cause immediate harm.

146. What is the primary purpose of a Public Key Infrastructure (PKI)?
A. To manage email servers and clients
B. To enable a wide range of dispersed people to communicate securely
C. To maintain a list of revoked driver's licenses
D. To ensure all websites are accessible without encryption

147. Which authentication method provides the weakest form of authentication?
A. HMAC
B. CBC-MAC
C. CMAC
D. Symmetric key-based MAC

148. What is the role of subkeys in the Cipher-Based Message Authentication Code (CMAC) process?
A. They are used to encrypt the entire message in one go.
B. They replace the need for a symmetric key.
C. They are used individually to encrypt the individual blocks of a message.
D. They are shared publicly to verify the integrity of the message.

149. What is the main reason for creating newer versions of hashing algorithms with larger message digest values?
A. To increase the speed of the hashing process
B. To reduce the size of the message

C. To improve resistance to brute-force attacks such as birthday attacks

D. To enable the encryption of larger messages

150. What is the primary goal of security models?

A. To design secure systems and architectures

B. To implement security policies

C. To conduct penetration testing

D. To monitor network traffic

151. What security protocol is commonly used for securing email communication?

A. IPsec

B. TLS/SSL

C. PGP

D. HTTPS

152. What is the result of the final block of ciphertext when using a Cipher Block Chaining Message Authentication Code (CBC-MAC)?
A. It is used as the MAC.
B. It is used as the initialization vector for the next message.
C. It is discarded to maintain message integrity.
D. It is encrypted again for extra security.

153. What is the major security concern that led to the development of SHA-2 and SHA-3 as successors to SHA-1?
A. Susceptibility to key recovery attacks
B. Vulnerability to collision attacks
C. Inability to be implemented in hardware
D. Lack of compatibility with digital certificates

154. Which of the following is NOT a function of a Message Authentication Code (MAC)?
A. Data encryption
B. Providing data origin authentication
C. Integrity checking
D. Detecting unauthorized message modifications


155. What does a Hash-based Message Authentication Code (HMAC) use in addition to the original message to ensure integrity and authentication?
A. A symmetric key
B. A public key
C. A parity bit
D. A digital certificate


156. Why are parity bits not suitable for detecting intentional unauthorized modifications to data?
A. They can be easily decrypted by attackers.
B. They do not provide confidentiality of the message.
C. They can be recalculated by an intruder to match altered data.
D. They are based on a secret hashing algorithm.


157. What does the term "zero-knowledge proof" imply in the context of cryptography?

A. That no information can be encrypted.
B. That the verifier can prove possession of a private key to others.
C. That the prover can demonstrate knowledge of a secret without revealing it.
D. That the encryption used is unbreakable.


158. What is the primary goal of misuse case testing in software development?

A. To improve user experience
B. To identify potential ways adversaries might subvert code

C. To ensure the software runs efficiently

D. To reduce the cost of software maintenance

159. Software controls are designed with various objectives. Which of the following is NOT a goal of software controls?

A. Controlling input

B. Facilitating malicious access

C. Managing encryption

D. Regulating interprocess communication

160. What is the relationship between functionality and security in software development?

A. Functionality is prioritized over security

B. Security is prioritized over functionality

C. Functionality and security are always equally important

D. Functionality and security do not influence each other

161. Which of the following best describes the phrase "hard and crunchy on the outside and soft and chewy on the inside" in a security context?

A. A software development methodology

B. An ideal security posture

C. A description of robust internal security environments

D. For strong perimeter security with weak internal protections

162. Why do many developers not practice implementing security during the software development stages?

A. It's not required by law

B. Security implementation is an outdated practice

C. It was not historically considered crucial

D. Customers don't demand security

163. Why is software often released with vulnerabilities?

A. There is a lack of understanding of security needs
B. Because customers demand quick releases over secure software
C. Because developers intentionally include vulnerabilities
D. Due to a lack of available security patches

164. What is the ideal default security setting for a newly installed security application or device?

A. Full access for user convenience
B. Partial access with some user permissions
C. No access until explicitly granted
D. Custom access based on vendor recommendations

165. Why do out-of-the-box implementations of software tend to be insecure?

A. Due to programming errors
B. complexity of security configurations
C. Vendors prioritize user friendliness and functionality.
D. lack of security knowledge among vendors

166. What is a common reason for the existence of unpatched systems?

A. Patches are too expensive
B. Administrators are not aware of the patches
C. There are no patches available for certain systems
D. Patches install automatically without administrator intervention

167. What is the ultimate solution to reducing the need for security patches?

A. Removing all security controls
B. Developing software properly in the first place
C. Relying on perimeter security devices like firewalls
D. Educating users about security risks

168. What is the primary purpose of the Software Development Life Cycle (SDLC)?
A. To ensure the software is developed quickly
B. To provide a structure for the unpredictability in software development
C. To ensure that software meets functionality, cost, quality, and delivery schedule requirements
D. To make software development more complex

169. Which of the following is NOT one of the main phases of the SDLC?
A. Operations and maintenance
B. Design
C. Deployment
D. Attack surface analysis

170. During which phase of the SDLC should a security risk assessment first be carried out?
A. Development
B. Testing
C. Requirements gathering
D. Design

171. What is the primary output from the design phase of the SDLC?
A. A complete and functional software product
B. A detailed project management plan
C. A design that outlines how the product will fulfill identified requirements
D. A fully tested software application

172. Which testing approach in the SDLC involves sending malformed or unexpected data to a software application to uncover vulnerabilities?
A. Unit testing
B. Fuzzing
C. Regression testing
D. Static analysis

173. In the context of the SDLC, what is the main goal of static analysis?
A. To simulate a range of inputs to which the code may be exposed
B. To examine code without executing the program to identify defects
C. To ensure the software runs in a production-like environment
D. To validate the final software against customer requirements

174. Which of the following phases of the SDLC involves deploying the software to a production environment?
A. Development
B. Operations and maintenance
C. Testing
D. Requirements gathering

175. What is the purpose of verification in the context of the SDLC?
A. To identify and reduce the attack surface of software
B. To ensure that the product meets the original specifications
C. To guarantee that the software is free of any vulnerabilities
D. To confirm that the software solves the intended real-world problem

176. What is a privacy impact rating used for in the SDLC?
A. To determine the cost/benefit ratio of security countermeasures
B. To indicate the sensitivity level of data processed by the software
C. To measure the software's performance in a production environment
D. To assess the effectiveness of the project management plan

177. What is the significance of a "zero-day" vulnerability in the context of the SDLC?

A. It is a vulnerability that is fixed on the same day it is discovered.
B. It is an unknown vulnerability with no pre-established fix.
C. It is a vulnerability only found in software that is one day old.
D. It refers to vulnerabilities discovered during the first phase of the SDLC.

178. Which software development methodology is known for its linear-sequential life-cycle approach, where each phase must be completed before the next one begins?

A. Agile
B. Spiral
C. V-shaped
D. waterfall

179. What is the primary emphasis of the V-shaped methodology in software development?

A. Rapid prototyping
B. Risk analysis
C. Verification and validation at each phase
D. Customer collaboration

180. Which of the following is NOT a type of prototyping model?

A. Rapid
B. Evolutionary
C. Operational
D. Static

181. In which methodology is a working version of the software produced after the first iteration and then improved upon in subsequent iterations?

A. Waterfall
B. Incremental
C. Spiral
D. RAD

182. The spiral methodology is best known for its focus on which aspect of software development?

A. Iterative development and prototyping
B. Emphasis on rapid development speed
C. Focus on user stories
D. Emphasis on risk analysis

183. What is a key feature of the Rapid Application Development (RAD) methodology?

A. Extensive upfront planning
B. Use of rapid prototyping
C. Rigid sequential development phases
D. Long development cycle

184. Which agile methodology is characterized by fixed-duration development intervals known as sprints?
A. Extreme Programming (XP)
B. Kanban
C. Scrum
D. Lean

185. What is the primary purpose of pair programming in Extreme Programming (XP)?
A. To increase development speed
B. To reduce the incidence of errors
C. To emphasize the importance of documentation
D. To follow a strict protocol

186. What is kanban primarily known for in the context of software development?
A. Its use of extensive and detailed documentation
B. Its emphasis on visual tracking of all tasks
C. Its reliance on heavy upfront design analysis
D. Its rigid development cycles

187. What is the goal of integrating DevOps practices in software development?
A. To separate the development and operations teams
B. To ensure that features are pushed out on strict schedules
C. To align the incentives of development, IT, and QA for more efficient releases

D. To follow a strict set of predefined processes

188. What is the primary purpose of Capability Maturity Model Integration (CMMI)?
A. To provide a set of guidelines for developing products and software.
B. To serve as a legal framework for software development contracts.
C. To offer financial assistance to software development companies.
D. To create a platform for social networking among software developers.

189. How can CMMI be used by customers when dealing with a software vendor?
A. To negotiate lower prices for software products.
B. To evaluate the vendor's security engineering practices.
C. To ensure the vendor uses the latest programming languages.
D. To demand faster delivery times for software development.

190. What is the outcome expected from a company that adheres to the CMMI model?
A. Decreased software quality due to standardization.
B. Longer life cycles for software development.
C. Improved software quality and better project management.
D. Increased reliance on individual heroics for success.

191. At which CMMI level are formal management structure and quality assurance processes initially established?
A. Initial
B. Repeatable
C. Defined
D. Managed

192. Which maturity model focuses on integrating development and operations teams?

A. Capability Maturity Model Integration.
B. DevOps Maturity Model.

C. Open Source Maturity Model.

D. Software Product Management Maturity Model.

193. What does the software product management maturity model emphasize?

A. The technical aspects of software development.

B. The integration of continuous improvement steps.

C. Business issues such as market conditions and product lines.

D. The use of artificial intelligence in software development.

194. What is the primary objective of change management in software development projects?

A. To ensure that changes are made randomly

B. To deliberately regulate the changing nature of projects

C. To eliminate the need for any changes during the project lifecycle

D. To allow all stakeholders to make changes at will

195. What should be done to source code changes before they are applied to production?

A. Directly implemented into production.

B. They should be made on the test version and bypass the librarian.

C. They should be made on the test version, documented, and tested.

D. They should be approved by the development team only.

196. What role does the librarian play in the change control process?

A. To test the new code

B. To make the actual code changes

C. To provide production code

D. To audit the system

197. Why is it important for customers to sign a contract confirming the agreed design and requirements?

A. To prevent the vendor from making any changes

B. To allow for unlimited changes without extra costs

C. To document the customer's agreement to the design and requirements

D. To ensure any further modifications are paid for by the customer

198. What can happen if change control is not properly put into place and enforced?

A. The project will always be completed on time.

B. The development team will have less work to do.

C. Scope creep can occur, leading to delays and financial losses.

D. The organization will become more efficient.

199. When a change request is made late in the development phase, what should the team leader do?

A. Ignore the change request.

B. Implement the change immediately.

C. Inform the project manager of the implications of the change.

D. Approve the change without consultation.

200. What could be a consequence of uncontrolled changes in a development team?

A. Increased compatibility between software pieces

B. A seamless integration of the product

C. Jobs may be in jeopardy due to unapproved changes.

D. Faster completion of the project

201. At what stage should a process for dealing with changes be established in a project?

A. After the first round of testing

B. Once the system audit is completed

C. At the beginning of the project

D. Only when the client requests changes

202. What are the necessary steps for a change control process?

A. Approval, implementation, testing

B. Requesting, analyzing, recording, submitting for approval, developing, reporting

C. Developing, testing, and deploying

D. Auditing, certifying, and accrediting

203. When might a system require another round of certification and accreditation?

A. When minor changes are made to the system

B. When the system is functioning well without issues

C. When significant changes are made to the system

D. When there is a change in the development team

204. Which of the following protocols is used for securely managing network devices such as routers and switches?

A. SNMPv1

B. SMTP

C. SSH

D. FTPS

205. What is the primary reason for avoiding giving software engineers unrestricted privileged access to their devices?

A. To encourage team collaboration

B. To ensure compliance with licensing

C. To enforce good change management practices

D. To reduce software development time

206. What is the recommended method for developers to access an isolated development network remotely?

A. Using direct connection over the internet

B. A virtual Private Network (VPN)

C. Unsecured Wi-Fi networks

D. Email attachments

207. What is a potential risk when an organization does not adequately isolate development and production systems?
A. Increased cost
B. Reduced collaboration
C. Compromised source code
D. Slower development cycles

208. What is the purpose of Software Configuration Management (SCM) in the software development life cycle?
A. To increase the speed of software development
B. To maintain software integrity and traceability
C. To simplify the development process
D. To reduce the need for testing

209. Which of the following is not a function provided by many SCM systems?

A. Concurrency management
B. Versioning and synchronization
C. Automatic code generation
D. Tracking revisions made by multiple people

210. What is the primary benefit of using an "Air-gapped" network for managing code repositories?
A. Enhance developer collaboration
B. Prevents unauthorized access to source code
C. To comply with software licensing agreements
D. To facilitate remote work practices

211. What is the role of Secure Shell (SSH) in securing code repositories?
A. It serves as a backup system for repository data.
B. It encrypts traffic within the intranet to mitigate the risk of sniffing.
C. It provides a user interface for code deployment.
D. It automatically compiles source code.

212. What is the purpose of software escrow?
A. To facilitate easier collaboration between companies
B. To provide a backup of the source code in case the vendor goes out of business
C. To reduce the cost of software development
D. To ensure compliance with software licensing

213. Why might a vendor be hesitant to hand over source code to a customer who paid for its development?
A. It might give away trade secrets or intellectual property
B. It would reveal the identity of the developers
C. The code is not valuable
D. It would require additional support and maintenance


214. Which of the following is not included in the OWASP Top 10 list of web application security risks as of 2017?
A. Insecure Deserialization
B. Broken Authentication
C. Sensitive Data Exposure
D. Remote Code Execution

215. What is the main goal of secure coding practices?
A. To make software development faster
B. To create aesthetically pleasing software interfaces
C. To develop software free from defects, especially exploitable ones
D. To adhere to the developer's personal coding preferences

216. Which organization is known for providing secure coding standards.
A. IEEE
B. OWASP
C. SEI
D. ISO/IEC

217. According to SEI's top 10 secure coding practices, what is the principle of "Default deny"?

A. Deny all requests unless explicitly required to allow them
B. Always allow requests by default
C. Deny all outputs from the system
D. Allow all inputs into the system without validation

218. Which algorithm is known for being more efficient than RSA and other asymmetric algorithms, particularly in devices with limited resources?

A. Diffie-Hellman
B. El Gamal
C. Elliptic Curve Cryptosystems (ECC)
D. Knapsack

219. What does the Public Key Infrastructure (PKI) rely on?

A. Symmetric key algorithms
B. Asymmetric key algorithms
C. One-way hash functions
D. Discrete logarithm problems

220. In the context of asymmetric algorithms, what is a one-way function?

A. A function that can only be computed in one direction.
B. A function that is used to generate public keys.
C. A function that encrypts data but cannot decrypt it.
D. A function that is used to authenticate a message sender.

221. Which one of these is not a part of the SEI's top 10 secure coding practices?

A. Using effective quality assurance techniques
B. Practicing defense in depth
C. Prioritizing high-performance code over secure code
D. Sanitizing data sent to other systems

222. What is considered the most primitive form of programming

language?
A. Assembly
B. High-level
C. Machine
D. Fourth-generation

223. What does assembly language use to represent machine-level instructions?
A. Binary codes
B. High-level statements
C. Mnemonics
D. Compilers

224. What is the main advantage of high-level programming languages?

A. They require extensive knowledge of computer architecture.
B. They allow direct control of very basic activities within a computer system.
C. They are easier to work with and more similar to human languages.
D. They are hardware-specific and not portable.

225. What is a primary feature of fourth-generation programming languages?

A. Direct control of hardware
B. Less manual coding for specific tasks
C. Symbolic representation of machine-level instructions
D. Non-portability

226. What is the goal of fifth-generation programming languages?
A. To eliminate the need for programming expertise
B. To increase the need for manual memory management
C. To focus on machine-level programming
D. To depend on assembly language for execution

227. What do compilers do?

A. They convert high-level language statements into machine code.

B. They translate mnemonics into high-level language.

C. They directly execute high-level code.

D. They interpret bytecode into high-level language.

228. What is the major disadvantage of using an interpreted programming language?

A. It allows for direct control of hardware.

B. It cannot run as a stand-alone application without an interpreter.

C. It requires extensive knowledge of computer architecture.

D. It is hardware-specific and not portable.

229. What is the concept of garbage collection in programming?

A. The manual process of deallocating memory blocks.

B. The process of optimizing assembly code.

C. An automated way to manage memory by deallocating blocks no longer in use.

D. A technique to improve the portability of code.

230. In Object-Oriented Programming (OOP), what is an object?

A. A high-level statement for abstraction

B. A machine code instruction set

C. An instance of a class

D. A tool like a compiler or interpreter

231. What advantage does low coupling have in software modules?

A. It requires interaction with many other modules.

B. It signifies that a module can carry out multiple tasks.

C. It makes modules easier to understand and reuse.

D. It represents the module's capability to execute complex tasks.

232. What was the Distributed Computing Environment (DCE) primarily developed for?

A. To provide a proprietary client/server framework for Microsoft

B. To standardize heterogeneous system communication through a client/server model

C. To provide a cloud computing model for Software-As-A-Service (SaaS)

D. To enable the development of mainframe computer systems

233. What does the directory service in DCE provide?

A. A list of available web services

B. Host clock synchronization

C. Network address and other information when given a name

D. A machine-readable description of web service operations

234. What is the purpose of Object Request Brokers (ORBs) in CORBA?

A. To provide a directory service for clients

B. To manage all communications between components in a distributed environment

C. To offer security services like authentication and authorization

D. To synchronize host clocks for event scheduling

235. What does DCOM stand for?

A. Direct Component Object Model

B. Distributed Component Object Model

C. Data Communication Object Model

D. Dynamic Component Object Model

236. What is the key advantage of using SOAP in distributed computing?

A. It is a proprietary protocol used only for Microsoft products

B. It uses XML and HTTP, which are standard web formats

C. It provides a service broker for locating services

D. It is the underlying technology for ActiveX components

237. Which technology is described as a framework for developing enterprise software mainly in the Java programming language?

A. CORBA

B. DCE

C. Java EE

D..NET framework

238. What is the primary function of Service-Oriented Architecture (SOA)?

A. To provide a single electrical power grid for home computing
B. To offer standardized access to services for various applications
C. To enable local personal computer sharing
D. To synchronize host clocks across a network

239. Which of the following is NOT a component of web services in SOA?

A. SOAP
B. WSDL
C. UDDI
D. DCOM

240. What is the purpose of UDDI in an SOA environment?
A. To encode messages for web services
B. To register and locate available services
C. To act as a middleware for distributed processing
D. To provide real-time priority scheduling

241. How do.NET framework applications execute?
A. On a local personal computer
B. Within an application virtual machine
C. Directly on the operating system
D. Through a centralized mainframe system

242. What is the main purpose of mobile code?
A. To provide additional content for web pages
B. To enhance the performance of the operating system
C. To serve as a platform for launching attacks
D. To protect the system from malicious activities

243. What makes Java platform-independent?

A. Its ability to create machine-level code directly
B. The use of Java Virtual Machine (JVM)

C. Its compilation into object code for specific operating systems

D. Its exclusive use of ActiveX controls

244. What is an applet in Java?

A. A full-fledged programming language

B. A small component designed to run in a user's web browser

C. A type of processor-specific machine code

D. A security mechanism to protect the system

245. What is the purpose of the sandbox in Java's security model?

A. To increase the performance of Java applets

B. To mediate access to system resources and limit the applet's activities

C. To authenticate user actions in the web browser

D. To compile Java source code into bytecode

246. How can Java applets pose a security risk?

A. They can only run in controlled environments

B. They cannot access system resources at all

C. They can accidentally or purposefully carry out malicious activity

D. They are always digitally signed and secure

247. What is ActiveX primarily used for?

A. To run Java applets in a web browser

B. To create self-sufficient programs executed in the Windows environment

C. To compile bytecode into machine-level code

D. To authenticate Java applets

248. What is one of the main security issues with ActiveX controls?

A. They cannot be downloaded from websites

B. They are always executed within a sandbox

C. They have the same privilege levels as the current user

D. They are not part of the Windows operating system

249. What is the main security difference between Java applets and ActiveX controls?
A. ActiveX controls are platform-independent
B. Java applets do not use digital certificates
C. Java applets execute within a sandbox, while ActiveX controls rely on digital certificates
D. ActiveX controls are not reusable

250. Why has Microsoft stopped supporting ActiveX in its Edge web browser?
A. Because it wasn't compatible with Java applets
B. Due to the platform-independent nature of ActiveX
C. Because of the security flaws inherent in ActiveX technology
D. ActiveX was too difficult for users to understand

251. Which two ports must typically be opened on a company's firewall to allow web-based traffic?
A. 22 and 23
B. 80 and 443
C. 21 and 22
D. 25 and 110

252. When developing a web application, what is the benefit of using off-the-shelf software compared to in-house developed applications?
A. It is more secure.
B. It offers more customization.
C. It eliminates all vulnerabilities.
D. It may have been tested with security in mind.

253. What is a significant risk associated with using web-based administrative interfaces?
A. They provide a convenient way for web admins to work from any

location.

B. They can only be accessed using secure channels.

C. They can be an entry point for unauthorized users.

D. They are required for managing web applications.

254. What is a common method that attackers use to obtain usernames for targeted systems?

A. Multi-factor authentication

B. Mining usernames via search engines

C. Social engineering attacks, such as phishing emails or phone calls, to trick users into revealing their usernames.

D. Brute-force attacks, where attackers use automated tools to systematically guess usernames until they find a valid one

255. What type of attack involves inserting characters like "../" into a URL to access directories that should not be accessible from the web?

A. SQL injection

B. Cross-Site Scripting (XSS)

C. Path or directory traversal

D. Session hijacking

256. What is the best practice for exchanging all authentication information over the web?

A. Using cookies

B. Encrypting the channel of communication via TLS

C. Utilizing session IDs

D. Implementing client-side validation

257. Which of the following is an input validation attack that uses a standard coding format to bypass validation rules?

A. Brute-force attack

B. Unicode encoding

C. Parameter tampering

D. Session fixation

258. How a non-persistent (reflected) XSS vulnerability does differs from a

persistent (stored) XSS vulnerability.
A. It does not require user interaction.
B. It occurs when an attacker's script is stored on the server.
C. It is executed on the server side.
D. It occurs when a user processes a URL with a rogue script.

259. What is the purpose of cookies in session management for web applications?
A. To encrypt communication between the client and server
B. To keep track of the state of a user's connection
C. To authenticate users with the server
D. To store sensitive user information

260. What is the principle of "failing securely" in web application design?

A. The application should allow all user behavior without displaying errors.
B. The application should only fail when under a cyber attack.
C. The application should display detailed error messages for debugging.
D. The application should handle errors without exposing system details.

261. What is the primary role of a Database Management System (DBMS)?
A. To provide a user-friendly interface for databases
B. To manage and control the security parameters of the database
C. To create a backup of the database regularly
D. To ensure network connectivity for remote user access

262. Which database model is most widely used today and presents information in the form of tables?
A. Hierarchical
B. Network
C. Relational
D. Object-oriented

263. What is the purpose of a primary key in a relational database?

A. To establish relationships between different databases

B. To link all the data within a record to a unique value

C. To define the database schema

D. To provide an interface for user interaction

264. Which of the following is NOT a characteristic of a database?

A. Providing transaction persistence

B. Allowing data sharing with multiple users

C. Supporting only one user at a time

D. Enforcing security controls for integrity checking

265. What is the key feature of an Object-Oriented Database (OODB)?

A. It uses SQL for all interactions

B. It stores data in two-dimensional tables

C. Data and procedures (methods) are bundled together.

D. It employs a strict tree structure for data organization

266. What does "polyinstantiation" enable in a database context?

A. Creation of multiple databases for redundancy

B. Multiple tuples with the same primary keys distinguished by security levels

C. A single instance of an object with varying attributes

D. Reducing the size of the database by eliminating redundant data

267. What is a data dictionary used for in a database?

A. To store backup copies of the database

B. To act as a central repository of data elements and their relationships

C. To maintain user access logs

D. To provide a virtual environment for testing queries

268. What is the main purpose of using roles in database security?

A. To simplify user account management

B. To provide direct access to the database

C. To streamline access control and restrict indirect database access

D. To allow unrestricted access to the database for auditing purposes

269. What are the four components of the ACID test that ensure reliable transaction processing in databases?
A. Assembly, Consistency, Isolation, Duration
B. Atomicity, Consistency, Isolation, Durability
C. Authentication, Confidentiality, Integrity, Durability
D. Accuracy, Consistency, Isolation, Documentation

270. Which of the following is NOT a common method by which malware can spread?
A. Sharing media
B. Downloading from the internet
C. Manual attacks on systems
D. Using encrypted messaging apps

271. What is the main purpose of a rootkit?
A. To encrypt user files for ransom
B. To provide the attacker with administrator-level access to a system
C. To serve advertisements to users
D. To act as a self-replicating virus

272. Which type of malware requires a host application to replicate?
A. Worm
B. Rootkit
C. Virus
D. Trojan horse

273. What is a characteristic of a polymorphic virus?
A. It hides its presence on a system
B. It can produce varied but operational copies of itself
C. It installs itself as part of the system kernel
D. It acts as a legitimate program but performs malicious actions in the background

274. What is a common use for botnets?
A. Enhancing system security

B. Performing Distributed Denial-of-Service (DDoS) attacks

C. Encrypting files for legitimate backup purposes

D. Providing free computational resources

275. What is the main difference between a virus and a worm?

A. A virus requires user action or intervention to spread, such as executing an infected file, whereas a worm can spread independently without user action.

B. A virus attaches itself to a host file or program and requires the host file to be executed to spread, while a worm is a standalone program that can replicate and spread independently

C. A virus typically infects a single computer or file system, while a worm can propagate across networks and infect multiple systems.

D. A virus often remains dormant until triggered by a specific event or action, whereas a worm is active as soon as it enters a system and begins replicating immediately

276. What technique do antimalware programs use to detect new, previously unknown malware?

A. Signature-based detection

B. Heuristic detection

C. Immunization

D. Manual code review

277. Which of the following is NOT a function typically performed by a rootkit?

A. Encrypting user files

B. Installing backdoor access

C. Capturing credentials

D. Removing traces from system logs

278. What is spyware primarily used for?

A. To display advertisements

B. To gather sensitive information about a user

C. To replicate itself via email

D. To create botnets

279. What is the purpose of Bayesian filtering in spam detection?
A. To encrypt messages for secure delivery
B. To detect and filter out unsolicited junk emails
C. To spread malware via email
D. To provide detailed statistics on email usage

280. What should every workstation, server, and mobile device have installed, according to the antimalware policy standards?
A. Firewall protection
B. Antivirus software
C. Antimalware software
D. Data loss prevention software

281. How often should antimalware policies and procedures be reviewed?
A. Monthly
B. Quarterly
C. Annually
D. Bi-annually

282. What type of files contain updates for antimalware software?
A. EXE files
B. DAT files
C. DLL files
D. ZIP files

283. Where can antimalware solutions be implemented to scan incoming traffic?
A. Email clients
B. Desktop environments
C. Network entry points
D. Virtual machines

284. What should be the frequency of virus scans on systems to ensure protection?

A. Only when the system is idle
B. Weekly
C. Manually as needed
D. Automated and scheduled

285. What is a critical aspect of assessing the security of acquired software?

A. The color scheme of the software interface
B. Vendor's reputation and regularity of patch updates
C. The number of features the software has
D. The price of the software

286. What is a key element in assessing the security of acquired software if the source code is not available?
A. User interface design
B. Penetration testing
C. Number of users
D. Software's age

287. What is an indicator of a risky vendor when acquiring software?
A. Large and well-established companies
B. Vendors with a limited market presence
C. Vendors with mature and documented development processes
D. Small or new companies with immature or undocumented development processes

288. What can organizations do to mitigate the risk of acquired software if they cannot perform code reviews or penetration tests?
A. Deploy the software widely with default configurations
B. Limit the software to specific subnetworks with hardened configurations
C. Disregard the need for intrusion detection/prevention systems
D. Fully trust the vendor's assurances without verification

289. What should users do if they discover a virus, as per the antimalware information and expected user behaviors?
A. Ignore the issue

B. Attempt to remove the virus themselves

C. Contact the designated person in the organization

D. Reboot their device

290. What is the main goal of the operations department in the context of security?

A. To ensure maximum profitability

B. To maintain a necessary level of security

C. To create new company policies

D. To focus solely on technological advancements

291. The concepts of due care and due diligence in a corporate setting are comparable to what?

A. A legal contract

B. A prudent person

C. An insurance policy

D. A business transaction

292. What are companies and senior executives legally obligated to ensure?

A. That profits are maximized

B. That employee satisfaction is high

C. That resources are protected and security measures are tested

D. That all employees have clear career paths

293. What can happen if operational security responsibilities are not met?

A. The company may receive an award

B. The company may face legal consequences

C. The company may be exempt from taxes

D. The company may be eligible for government grants

294. What types of threats must an organization consider?

A. Natural disasters and employee turnover

B. Product defects and market competition

C. Disclosure of confidential data and corruption of data

D. Changes in management and public relations issues

295. What does it mean when a system or operation is considered sensitive?

A. It needs to be protected from disclosure

B. It should be open to the public

C. It is outdated and needs replacement

D. It is used for marketing purposes

296. Which of the following is NOT a concern of operational security?

A. Configuration management

B. Employee hiring processes

C. Fault tolerance

D. Security

297. What does a critical system or operation imply?

A. It must be cost-effective

B. It must remain available at all times

C. It must be the latest technology

D. It is optional for the company's operations

298. What physical and environmental concerns does operational security address?

A. Corporate branding and image

B. Temperature and humidity controls

C. Office interior design

D. Travel arrangements for executives

299. Operational security is about managing which of the following?

A. Only the company's finances

B. Only the company's legal affairs

C. Configuration, performance, fault tolerance, security, and accounting

D. Just the IT infrastructure

300. What is the main drawback of the El Gamal algorithm when compared to other asymmetric algorithms?
A. It is less secure.
B. It can only be used for key exchange.
C. It is slower in performance.
D. It does not provide encryption functionality.

301. What is the benefit of job rotation in a company?
A. It allows for continuous work without breaks
B. It helps to identify suspicious activities
C. It increases the network's performance
D. It allows users to set their security profiles

302. Which attack is the Diffie-Hellman algorithm particularly vulnerable to?

A. Brute force
B. Side-channel
C. Man-in-the-middle
D. Time-memory trade-off

303. What is the primary advantage of using RSA over other asymmetric algorithms?
A. It is based on discrete logarithms.
B. It can be used for digital signatures, key exchange, and encryption.
C. It uses smaller key sizes.
D. It is the fastest algorithm.

304. Why should the security administrator not report to the network administrator?
A. They are responsible for enforcing mandatory vacations
B. They handle all user requests for password resets
C. Their focus on security could conflict with the network administrator's aim for performance
D. They are solely responsible for implementing and maintaining access control mechanisms

305. Who is responsible for implementing and maintaining security devices and software?
A. The network administrator
B. The computer user
C. The security administrator
D. All employees

306. What is the purpose of reviewing audit logs?
A. To determine network performance
B. To detect unauthorized access attempts and other security issues
C. To set initial passwords for users
D. To implement security labels in MAC environments

307. What is authorization creep?
A. A routine method for auditing user activities
B. A baseline for violation activities set by clipping levels
C. The gradual accumulation of unnecessary user permissions
D. The process of rotating job roles among employees

308. What is one of the questions administrators should ask when monitoring users?

A. Should network performance be prioritized over security?
B. Are users performing tasks necessary for their job description?
C. How can mandatory vacations be enforced?
D. Should security devices be set and forgotten?

309. What are clipping levels?

A. Devices that control user access to resources
B. Predefined types of acceptable errors or violations
C. Training programs for new security administrators
D. The maximum number of tasks an employee can perform

310. What is the primary purpose of implementing a layered approach to physical security?

A. To reduce costs associated with security measures
B. To ensure that if one security layer fails, there are no other protective measures
C. To provide multiple barriers to deter or delay an intruder before reaching sensitive areas
D. To make it easier for employees to access restricted areas

311. Why is it important to have a diversity of controls in physical security?
A. To make the security system more complex and confusing for security personnel
B. To ensure that if an intruder obtains one key, they can access all areas
C. To provide a single point of failure for easier maintenance
D. To prevent an intruder from having widespread access if they compromise one control

312. What is the role of personnel within sensitive areas as part of physical security controls?
A. To provide an audit trail of their actions
B. To personally detect and report suspicious behavior
C. To maintain and repair security devices as needed
D. To operate surveillance cameras at all times

313. When considering physical security measures, why should locks not be the sole protection scheme?
A. Locks are aesthetic features that do not provide real security
B. Locks can be picked or broken, and keys can be lost or duplicated
C. Locks are too expensive to implement on all doors.
D. Locks do not provide a way to monitor who is accessing an area.

314. What are cipher locks?
A. Traditional locks that require a physical key
B. Keyless and use keypads or swipe cards to control access
C. Less secure as they can be easily hacked
D. Only used in residential properties for basic security.

315. What is the purpose of door delay functionality in cipher combination locks?
A. To lock the door immediately after it is closed
B. To trigger an alarm if a door is held open for too long
C. To delay unauthorized personnel from entering
D. To provide a time buffer for security personnel to arrive

316. Which of the following is NOT a characteristic commonly available on many cipher combination locks?
A. Key override
B. Master keying
C. Hostage alarm
D. Automatic relocking after a set time

317. Why should the combination of locks be changed periodically?

A. To ensure the locks do not rust over time
B. To prevent intruders from guessing worn or frequently used keys
C. To comply with insurance policy requirements
D. To ensure security personnel remain actively involved by introducing new combinations regularly.

318. What is the primary purpose of implementing bollards around a building?
A. To enhance the aesthetic appearance of the property
B. To provide seating for visitors and employees
C. To deter vehicles from driving through exterior walls
D. To serve as a guide for pedestrian traffic

319. What should be included in the audit trail for physical access control systems?
A. Only successful access attempts
B. Date and time of access attempts only
C. User ID employed and the entry point used for the attempt
D. Details of the security guard on duty at the time of access

320. What does the term 'provisioning' mean in the context of the CISSP exam?
A. The process of running wires and setting up networks
B. The acquisition and configuration of a new server
C. Automatically, a new instance of a physical server
D. The set of all activities required to provide new information services to users


321. Why is asset inventory a critical control in securing information systems?

A. It is required for financial reporting purposes
B. It simplifies the procurement process
C. It helps in tracking the physical location of hardware
D. It helps identify what needs to be defended in the organization


322. What is a primary security concern when tracking hardware in an organization?
A. Overestimating the value of the hardware
B. Difficulty in physically locating the hardware
C. Potential presence of back doors or piracy issues in hardware assets
D. Ensuring that the hardware matches the company's brand image

323. What is a recommended best practice for tracking software within an organization?

A. Conducting regular manual audits of software installations
B. Allowing users to install any software they prefer
C. Implementing application whitelisting
D. Purchasing additional software licenses as a buffer


324. What does the asset management life cycle begin with?
A. The retirement of the old asset
B. Identification of a new requirement

C. Operation phase

D. Acquisition from a vendor

325. What is the main purpose of a change management board?

A. To procure new software licenses

B. To ensure new assets do not introduce undue risks

C. To track the physical location of hardware

D. To oversee the retirement of assets

326. Which of the following is NOT a type of cloud service model?

A. Infrastructure-as-a-Service (IaaS)

B. Platform-as-a-Service (PaaS)

C. Software-as-a-Service (SaaS)

D. Hardware-as-a-Service (HaaS)

327. In the context of media management, why should a report be generated even when there is "no output"?

A. To ensure that the system is still functioning correctly

B. To confirm that the task was carried out despite no new data

C. To prevent the media from being unused

D. To maintain a consistent schedule for reporting

328. What is the primary goal of configuration management in terms of system security?

A. To ensure systems operate efficiently for business purposes

B. To establish and maintain consistent baselines on all systems

C. To update software applications regularly

D. To facilitate the user's ability to configure their systems

329. When is a system reboot typically triggered?

A. When the system detects a power surge

B. When there is a kernel failure, and the system shuts down in a controlled manner

C. When a user requests a manual restart

D. When there is a software update installation

330. What is the primary purpose of implementing RAID in a storage environment?

A. To decrease the overall storage capacity

B. To improve the physical security of the disks

C. To enhance the read-and-write performance and provide redundancy

D. To reduce energy consumption of storage devices

331. What is the term used to refer to the expected amount of time it will take to repair or replace a failed device and restore it to normal operation?

A. Mean Time Between Failures (MTBF)

B. Mean Time to Repair (MTTR)

C. Recovery Time Objective (RTO)

D. Recovery Point Objective (RPO)

332. Which of the following is most likely to be used in a high-availability environment where downtime cannot be tolerated?

A. Standard hard drives with a high MTBF

B. Fault-tolerant technologies

C. Basic redundant servers without hot swapping

D. Single-threaded CPU processors

333. What does the term 'single point of failure' refer to in a network environment?

A. A device that improves network performance

B. A device or system that, if it fails, will not affect the network's operation

C. A device or system that, if it fails, can bring down the entire network or a segment of it

D. The main server that hosts all network services

334. What does 'hot swapping' mean in the context of hardware redundancy?

A. Replacing hardware with the power turned off
B. Swapping out components without interrupting the system's operation
C. Upgrading the system hardware during maintenance of windows
D. Cooling down hardware components to prevent overheating.

335. Which RAID level is most used and involves striping with parity for fault tolerance?
A. RAID 0
B. RAID 1
C. RAID 5
D. RAID 10

336. What are Service Level Agreements (SLAs) primarily used for in IT operations?
A. Defining the project scope for new IT developments
B. Outlining the customer service policies of an IT department
C. Setting the expectations for the type and level of IT services provided
D. Detailing the training procedures for new IT personnel

337. What is the purpose of implementing redundant paths between routers in a network environment?

A. To increase the data transmission rate
B. To reduce the cost of network infrastructure
C. To prevent a single point of failure and ensure network availability
D. To simplify network topology

338. What is the main advantage of using Hierarchical Storage Management (HSM)?

A. It encrypts data for secure storage
B. It reduces storage costs by shifting rarely accessed data to cheaper storage media.
C. It increases the storage capacity of hard drives
D. It decreases the time required to access frequently used data

339. which of the following purposes is in server environments primarily used for which of the following purposes?
A. To provide a single operating system for multiple servers
B. To reduce the physical space required for server storage
C. To increase storage capacity without adding more disks
D. To improve system availability and provide load balancing

340. What is the primary difference between an Intrusion Detection System (IDS) and an Intrusion Prevention System (IPS)?
A. An IDS detects and stops intrusions, while an IPS only detects them.
B. Both IDS and IPS prevent intrusions by deploying honeypots.
C. An IPS detects and stops intrusions, while an IDS only detects them.
D. An IDS and an IPS are essentially the same, with no significant differences.

341. What is the primary advantage of using RSA over other asymmetric algorithms?

A. It is based on discrete logarithms.
B. It can be used for digital signatures, key exchange, and encryption.
C. It uses smaller key sizes.
D. It is the fastest algorithm.

342. Which of the following asymmetric algorithms is based on the difficulty of factoring large numbers?

A. Diffie-Hellman
B. El Gamal
C. RSA
D. ECC

343. What does NIST Special Publication 800-137, "Information Security Continuous Monitoring (ISCM)," define?
A. Patch management processes.
B. Guidelines for network architecture.
C. The practice of maintaining ongoing awareness of information security.
D. The process of identifying and responding to social engineering attacks.

344. Which of the following is considered a best practice for patch management?

A. Decentralized patching where each device independently checks for updates.

B. Centralized patch management with immediate deployment of patches.

C. Centralized patch management with testing before deployment.

D. Prohibiting patch updates to maintain configuration stability.

345. Why might an organization choose to outsource security operations to a Managed Security Services Provider (MSSP)?

A. To avoid the need for security policies and administrative controls.

B. MSSPs can always provide better security than in-house teams.

C. Due to a shortage of experienced security professionals and resource constraints.

D. MSSPs take on legal liability in case of a security breach.

346. What is the primary purpose of the Diffie-Hellman algorithm?

A. To encrypt messages

B. To generate digital signatures

C. To securely distribute symmetric keys

D. To factor large numbers into primes

347. What is vulnerability management?

A. A process to ensure that firewalls are deployed and configured properly.

B. The periodic testing of security controls using penetration tests.

C. A process of identifying, determining risks, and applying controls for vulnerabilities.

D. The deployment of honeypots and honeynets to collect threat intelligence.

348. What is the purpose of employing a safelist in network security?

A. To list known-bad resources such as malicious IP addresses or domains.

B. To set up decoy networks that attract attackers for observation.

C. To contain a set of known-good resources like IP addresses or applications.
D. To monitor and restrict the information that is flowing out of the network.

349. What is the role of baselining in the context of Intrusion Detection Systems (IDS)?
A. Baselining is used to determine the maximum throughput for IDS hardware.
B. It involves setting up honeypots to attract and monitor intrusions.
C. It is the process of establishing normal patterns of behavior for a network or system.
D. It refers to the use of sandboxes to test IDS configurations safely.

350. What is the first phase in the (ISC)²-prescribed seven phases of the incident management process?

A. Respond
B. Mitigate
C. Detect
D. Recover

351. Which department should manage an incident response policy?
A. Marketing
B. Security
C. Human Resources
D. Finance

352. What should an incident response team do first when a suspected crime is reported?

A. Contact law enforcement immediately
B. Inform senior management
C. Investigate to confirm if a crime has been committed
D. Document the events

353. What kind of team is composed of experts with other duties within the organization and might have slower response times?

A. Permanent
B. Virtual
C. Ad hoc
D. Hybrid

354. Which term describes one or more related events that negatively affect the company and impact its security posture?
A. Anomaly
B. Incident
C. Event
D. Breach

355. What is the main goal of incident handling?
A. To prosecute the attackers
B. To contain and mitigate any damage caused by an incident
C. To encrypt data
D. To monitor network traffic

356. What is the last phase in the incident management process?
A. Report
B. Learn
C. Remediate
D. Recover

357. According to the cyber kill chain model, what is the stage called when the malicious software establishes communication with the attackers?

A. Weaponization
B. Delivery
C. Installation
D. Command and Control (C&C)

358. What is a proactive measure in incident management?

A. Incident reporting
B. Log aggregation and SIEM
C. Remediation
D. Legal counsel

359. Why is it essential to initially treat all security incidents as potential crime scenes?

A. To preserve the chain of custody for evidence
B. To ensure that malicious actors are immediately identified
C. A malicious actor could have caused the incident

D. To comply with federal and state laws

360. What is the 'chain of custody' in the context of computer investigations?
A. A documentation process that records who has handled the evidence
B. The process of collecting evidence from the crime scene
C. A chronological record of an incident response
D. The specific protocol for evidence destruction after a case is closed

361. Which of the following terms is used as a synonym for computer forensics, network forensics, electronic data discovery, cyber forensics, and forensic computing by (ISC)²?
A. Digital evidence analysis
B. Cyber investigation
C. Digital forensics
D. Information technology examination

362. What must a forensic investigator avoid when initially responding to an attacked system?
A. Rebooting the system
B. Documenting their actions
C. Collecting evidence in order of volatility
D. Working on a copy of the attacked system

363. According to the SWGDE principles, what is the responsibility of any

agency that seizes digital evidence?

A. To provide the evidence to law enforcement officials

B. To ensure compliance with the SWGDE principles

C. To immediately analyze the digital evidence

D. To document the technical aspects of the evidence

364. What encompasses Motive, Opportunity, and Means (MOM) in identifying computer criminals?

A. The suspect's technical skills, access rights, and behavioral patterns

B. The legal, technical, and ethical aspects of the investigation

C. The reason, chance, and capability related to the crime

D. The types of tools used, time of the attack, and the attacker's location

365. What is the first phase in the common investigation process of a forensic investigation?

A. Preservation

B. Identification

C. Collection

D. Analysis

366. What kind of evidence should be collected first due to its volatile nature?

A. Disk images

B. Network logs

C. Process tables

D. Registers and cache

367. What is a crucial element in establishing that a computer user has no right to privacy when using company equipment?

A. Employee consent forms

B. Regular security audits

C. Legal banners upon system login

D. A company's acceptable use policy

368. What is the primary difference between enticement and entrapment in the context of capturing a suspect's actions?

A. Entrapment is legal, but enticement is not

B. Entrapment is ethical, but enticement is not

C. Entrapment tricks a person into committing a crime they had no intention of committing

D. Entrapment relies on passive monitoring, while enticement involves direct interaction

369. What is the purpose of a Recovery Time Objective (RTO) in disaster recovery planning?

A. To determine the maximum time a company can operate without a particular system

B. To calculate the financial impact of a disaster

C. To identify the minimum amount of data that must be restored after a disaster

D. To decide the maximum acceptable downtime for business processes after a disaster

370. What does the Recovery Point Objective (RPO) indicate in disaster recovery?

A. The specific moment when systems need to be returned to their normal functioning state.

B. The amount of data that can be permanently lost

C. The acceptable amount of data loss measured in time

D. The time it takes to recover from a disaster

371. Which of the following best describes the Work Recovery Time (WRT)?

A. The time to complete a full data backup

B. The time needed to restore and test systems after RTO is met

C. The duration for which a business can function without its main facility

D. The time it takes to assess the damage caused by a disaster

372. What is a hot site in the context of disaster recovery?

A. A location prone to disasters like fires and earthquakes
B. A facility fully configured and ready to operate within a few hours
C. A backup office space that only provides basic utilities
D. An offsite storage place for backup tapes and documents

373. Which block cipher is known for its flexibility in terms of variable block size, key size, and number of rounds?
  A. IDEA
  B. RC4
  C. RC5
  D. RC6

374. What role does Maximum Tolerable Downtime (MTD) play in business continuity planning?

A. It defines the acceptable delay in data restoration
B. It determines the duration a company can survive without specific operations
C. It calculates the cost of downtime for a company
D. It identifies the critical data that must be backed up

375. Which site is considered the cheapest option for disaster recovery but takes the longest to become operational?

A. Hot site
B. Warm site
C. Cold site
D. Redundant site

376. In the event of a disaster, what is the purpose of electronic vaulting?

A. To encrypt data for secure storage
B. To transmit bulk data to an offsite backup location
C. To maintain power supplies during outages
D. To physically transport backup tapes to a secure facility

377. What is the primary function of a service bureau in a disaster recovery

context?

A. To provide legal assistance during a disaster
B. To offer additional space and capacity for applications and services
C. To dispatch emergency services to a disaster site
D. To serve as a public relations firm during a disaster

378. Which of the following best defines a reciprocal agreement in a disaster recovery plan?

A. A contract with a third-party vendor for offsite data storage
B. An agreement between two companies to use each other's facilities in case of a disaster
C. A legal arrangement with local authorities for emergency response
D. A mutual contract with software vendors for continued service support

379. What is the primary purpose of conducting due diligence?

A. To create legal contracts with third-party vendors
B. To investigate all aspects of a business before a purchase
C. To implement the best fire detection and suppression systems
D. To provide online banking functionality to customers

380. What could be the consequence for a company if it fails to perform due diligence and due care?
A. Increased customer satisfaction
B. Potential criminal charges and civil suits
C. Improved market share and reputation
D. Enhanced security mechanisms

381. The "proximate cause" in legal terms refers to the direct reason or factor that led to a particular outcome or event.

A. The total amount of financial loss a company suffers
B. An act or omission that naturally and directly produces a consequence
C. The process of evaluating third-party security measures
D. The act of gathering information for decision-making

382. What is the effective key length of DES, considering the bits used for parity?

A. 64 bits
B. 56 bits
C. 128 bits
D. 32 bits

383. What is the importance of integrating security requirements into contractual agreements?

A. To ensure that security measures are not too costly
B. To allow easy termination of contracts
C. To ensure that legal, regulatory, and security requirements are covered
D. To guarantee a fixed profit margin

384. Which mode of DES operation is the fastest and easiest but may reveal patterns if used to encrypt large amounts of data?

A. Electronic Codebook (ECB)
B. Cipher Block Chaining (CBC)
C. Cipher Feedback (CFB)
D. Output Feedback (OFB)

385. What is the significance of vendor management?

A. To minimize the importance of vendors in business operations
B. To ensure performance metrics, SLAs, and reporting structures are upheld
C. To enable the company to shift all responsibility to the vendor
D. To reduce the frequency of meetings with vendors

386. Why is it important for an organization to consider insurance?

A. To increase the organization's profit margins
B. To cover the costs associated with the team outings
C. To protect against threats that cannot be prevented
D. To replace the need for a business impact analysis

387. What should the decision on whether to obtain insurance and the amount of coverage be based on?

A. The preference of the BCP team
B. The probability of the threat and the potential loss
C. The cost of the insurance premiums
D. The advice of the insurance agent

388. With whom should the BCP team collaborate to gain insight into existing insurance coverage and available options?

A. External stakeholders
B. The insurance company
C. Management
D. Customers and clients

389. What is the purpose of cyber insurance for companies?

A. To cover physical damages to company property
B. To insure losses caused by various cyber threats
C. To protect against employee theft
D. To ensure the company's vehicles

390. What kind of factors influence the premium of a company's cyber insurance policy?

A. The company's financial performance
B. The company's previous history of cyber incidents
C. The security measures in place like IDS, antivirus software, firewalls, etc.
D. The number of employees in the company

391. What does a business interruption insurance policy cover?

A. Expenses for marketing and advertising
B. Specified expenses and lost earnings if the company is out of business temporarily
C. All wages of employees, regardless of business operations
D. The cost of relocating the company

392. What type of insurance coverage can a company purchase to protect against uncollectible accounts receivable?
A. General liability insurance
B. Property insurance
C. Accounts receivable insurance
D. Workers' compensation insurance

393. What is an important aspect of understanding insurance policies for a company?

A. Memorizing the policy number
B. Knowing what is expected of the company and what is expected from the insurance provider
C. Predicting the exact amount of future claims
D. Choosing the policy with the most coverage regardless of cost

394. What is the primary function of access controls in computer security?
A. To increase system performance
B. To control how users and systems interact with resources
C. To provide encryption for data
D. To ensure compliance with software licensing

395. What is a subject in the context of access control?
A. A passive entity that contains information
B. The information flow between entities
C. An active entity that requests access to an object
D. A list of users and groups with access rights

396. What is an object in terms of access control?
A. A security protocol
B. An active entity requesting information
C. A passive entity containing information or functionality
D. The process of authenticating a user

397. What happens when a user logs in and attempts to access a file they are not authorized to view?

A. The file is automatically encrypted.
B. The user's permissions are upgraded.
C. The user is prompted to enter a password.
D. The user is denied access to the file.

398. What may users' permissions and rights be based on in an access control system?
A. Their identity, clearance, and group membership
B. The type of device they are using
C. The time of day they attempt to access
D. The physical location of the user

399. Which of the following is NOT a type of entity that may require access to network resources?
A. User
B. Database field
C. Computer program
D. Router

400. What is the result of successful authentication in the context of access control?

A. Immediate access to all system resources
B. Determination of the level of authorization
C. A temporary suspension of user rights
D. Activation of antivirus software

401. What is the role of access control concerning resource availability?
A. To distribute resources evenly among all users
B. To ensure all resources are public
C. To control, restrict, monitor, and protect resource availability
D. To provide unlimited access to resources

402. Which mode of operation for block ciphers does not reveal a pattern because it incorporates dependence between blocks?

A. Electronic Code Book (ECB)
B. Cipher Block Chaining (CBC)
C. Cipher Feedback (CFB)
D. Counter (CTR)

403. What is the significance of a file with a list of users and groups with the right to access it?
A. It indicates the file is encrypted.
B. It suggests that the file is available to everyone.
C. It is a form of access control.
D. It is a way to track file modifications.

404. What are the three main security principles?
A. Encryption, fault Tolerance, and Access Control
B. Authentication, authorization, and accounting
C. Availability, integrity, and confidentiality
D. Firewalls, antivirus, and intrusion detection systems

405. How many rounds of cryptographic functions does Blowfish utilize?
A. 8 rounds
B. 12 rounds
C. 16 rounds
D. 20 rounds

406. What is the block size that the Data Encryption Standard (DES) operates on?

A. 32-bit
B. 64-bit
C. 128-bit
D. 256-bit

407. Which example illustrates a breach of integrity?
A. A user's inability to access a file server due to downtime
B. An intercepted email that is altered without detection

C. Disclosure of financial account information to unauthorized individuals
D. Slow network speeds affecting file downloads

408. Which algorithm was selected by NIST to replace DES as the Advanced Encryption Standard (AES)?

A. MARS
B. Serpent
C. Twofish
D. Rijndael

409. Which of the following is NOT an example of a mechanism to provide confidentiality?
A. Encryption
B. Database views
C. Fault tolerance
D. Logical and physical access controls

410. Why is identifying the sensitivity of data critical for confidentiality?

A. To ensure all data receives the same level of security
B. To avoid spending unnecessary time and money on less critical data
C. To make data recovery processes simpler
D. To facilitate easier access to all data

411. Which of the following is NOT a characteristic of a strong stream cipher?
A. Long periods of no repeating patterns within keystream values
B. A keystream statistically biased in favor of zeroes
C. A keystream, not linearly related to the key
D. Easy to implement in hardware

412. What is the purpose of using Initialization Vectors (IVs) in encryption?
A. To speed up the encryption process
B. To reduce the size of the ciphertext

C. To prevent the creation of patterns during encryption

D. To replace the need for keys

413. Which security mechanism is specifically used in protecting trade secrets and financial transactions?

A. Antivirus software

B. Firewalls

C. Virtual Private Networks (VPNs)

D. Intrusion detection systems

414. What is the process by which a system verifies the identity of a subject?

A. Authorization

B. Accountability

C. Authentication

D. Identification

415. Which of the following is NOT a general factor used for authentication?

A. Something a person, knows

B. Something, a person, has

C. Something, a person, is

D. Something a person imagines

416. What type of error in a biometric system refers to when an authorized individual is incorrectly rejected?

A. Type I error

B. Type II error

C. Crossover error

D. Logical error

417. In identity management, what is an authoritative source of identity information called?

A. Identity Management (IdM)
B. Identity and Access Management (IAM)
C. Authoritative System of Record (ASOR)
D. Credential Management System (CMS)

418. What does the acronym MAC stand for in the context of access control within a network protocol stack?
A. Message Authentication Code
B. Media Access Control
C. Mandatory Access Control
D. Multifactor Authentication Code

419. What is the purpose of the crossover error rate in biometric systems?
A. To represent the point when the system must be reset
B. To indicate when the system's accuracy is at its lowest
C. To measure when the false rejection rate equals the false acceptance rate
D. To calculate the average error rate of the system

420. What is a race condition in the context of software security?
A. When a software process is terminated unexpectedly
B. When two or more processes use a shared resource in an incorrect order
C. When a software process runs faster than it is designed to
D. When software functions are executed in the correct sequence

421. What is the result of strong authentication in a security process?

A. Using one method of authentication
B. Using only a password for authentication
C. Using more than one authentication method

D. Using a simple PIN code

422. What does the uniqueness requirement ensure in the context of digital identities within a directory service?

A. Each user must have the same ID for accountability

B. Each user must have a unique ID for accountability

C. Each user ID should indicate the purpose of that account

D. Each user ID should be shared between users

423. What does a logical access control enforce in a computer security context?

A. Physical barriers to prevent unauthorized access

B. Identification and authentication procedures in hardware components

C. Technical measures for identification, authentication, authorization, and accountability

D. The physical presence of a person for access to be granted

424. What is Identity-as-a-Service (IDaaS)?

A. A cloud storage solution

B. A type of SaaS offering focused on identity management

C. An in-house server maintenance service

D. A hardware purchasing service

425. Which of the following is an example of an on-premise IdM system?

A. A system managed by a third-party service provider

B. A system where all needed resources remain under physical control of the enterprise

C. A cloud-based identity management system

D. A system that is always connected to the internet

426. What is a potential issue with using IDaaS in regulated industries?

A. Too much control over identity management

B. Inability to remain compliant due to outsourcing critical functions

C. Oversupply of unnecessary features

D. Lack of integration with internet services

427. When is an on-premise IdM solution most appropriate?
A. For managing identities for systems that are always online
B. When an organization wants to outsource its IdM
C. For managing identities for systems not directly connected to the internet
D. When an organization has no physical infrastructure

428. According to Gartner, what is the prediction for IDaaS by 2021?
A. More advanced technologies will replace it
B. The majority of new system purchases will use IDaaS
C. It will become less popular than on-premise solutions
D. It will be mandatory for all businesses

429. What is a critical requirement for establishing connectivity in IdM services?
A. Unlimited data transfer
B. High latency communication
C. Secure communication between components
D. Physical proximity of all components

430. What is a potential issue when establishing trust between nodes in identity services?
A. Nodes may not trust default Certificate Authorities (CAs)
B. Nodes do not require encryption
C. Nodes have unlimited trust in each other
D. Nodes only use pre-shared keys

431. What is the recommended approach for testing the integration of identity services?
A. Implementing the entire system at once
B. Rolling out to one department or division after testing with non-real users
C. Testing only in live production environments

D. Outsourcing the testing phase to external parties

432. Why is it crucial to integrate federated systems carefully when dealing with IdM?

A. Because federated systems do not require identity services
B. Because the cost of federated systems is typically higher
C. Because federated systems' dependencies may be complex and intertwined with external systems
D. Because federated systems are less secure than standalone systems

433. What is a session key?
A. A public key used for a single session.
B. A symmetric key is used for multiple sessions.
C. A symmetric key is used for a single session.
D. An asymmetric key used for key exchange.

434. What is the primary characteristic of Discretionary Access Control (DAC)?
A. Users are given access based on their security clearance level.
B. The operating system strictly enforces access based on predefined policies.
C. The owner of the resource specifies which subjects can access it.
D. The role within an organization determines access.

435. Which of the following is an example of Mandatory Access Control (MAC)?
A. A user with a 'secret' clearance is allowed to access 'top secret' documents.
B. An employee is given access to files based on their departmental role.
C. A system administrator assigns access permissions to users based on their job requirements.
D. A user cannot change permissions or install software due to strict system-enforced rules.

436. Which access control model allows for permissions to be managed in terms of user job roles?

A. Discretionary access control
B. Mandatory access control
C. Role-Based access control
D. Rule-based access control

437. What is the main difference between DAC and Rule-Based Access Control?
A. DAC is more flexible, while rule-based is more structured.
B. DAC is identity-based, while Rule-Based is not necessarily identity-based.
C. DAC uses security labels, while Rule-Based uses ACLs.
D. the system administrator enforces DAC, while the users enforce Rule-Based.

438. What is an example of a system that operates under Mandatory Access Control (Mac)?

A. Windows operating system
B. Linux operating system
C. SE Linux developed by the NSA
D. A typical personal computer

439. What is a characteristic feature of Hierarchical Role-Based Access Control (RBAC)?
A. It allows users to install software based on their role.
B. It provides role inheritance and reflects organizational structures.
C. It uses ACLs to enforce access control at the object level.
D. It is based on the discretion of the resource owner.

440. What is the main advantage of stream ciphers over block ciphers?
A. Better scalability for increased bandwidth
B. Higher level of security

C. More commonly used

D. No need for Initialization Vectors (IVs)

441. In which access control model does the 'Need-to-Know' rule apply?
A. Discretionary Access Control
B. Mandatory Access Control
C. Role-Based Access Control
D. Attribute-Based Access Control

442. What does the term 'sensitivity labels' refer to in the context of access control?
A. Labels that identify the owner of an object in DAC systems.
B. Labels that determine the operations a user can perform in RBAC systems.
C. Labels that contain classification and categories for enforcing access control in MAC systems.
D. Labels that specify rules for object access in RBAC systems.

443. Which access control mechanism provides the most granularity in defining access policies?
A. Discretionary Access Control
B. Mandatory Access Control
C. Role-Based Access Control
D. Attribute-Based Access Control

444. What is the primary function of constrained user interfaces?

A. To provide users with comprehensive system access

B. To restrict users' access abilities by limiting their functions or information

C. To enhance the user experience with customizable interfaces

D. To encrypt user communications for increased security

445. Which protocol uses TCP as its transport protocol?

A. RADIUS
B. Diameter
C. TACACS+
D. PAP

446. What does the acronym 'AAA' stand for in the context of remote access control technologies?

A. Authentication, Authorization, and Auditing
B. Authentication, Authorization, and Accounting
C. Authentication, Access, and Auditing
D. Authentication, Access, and Accounting

447. What is the major difference between ACLs and capability tables?

A. ACLs define what operations a subject can perform, while capability tables list objects a subject can access.
B. ACLs are bound to the object, whereas capability tables are bound to the subject.
C. Capability tables are used in network configurations, while ACLs are used in operating systems.
D. Capability tables provide encryption, while ACLs provide a list of authorized users.

448. Which of the following is a characteristic of, not shared by RADIUS?
A. It encrypts only the user's password during transmission.
B. It uses a true AAA architecture separating authentication, authorization, and accounting.
C. It is backward-compatible with previous versions.
D. It uses UDP as its transport protocol.

449. What is the diameter protocol designed to provide?
A. A replacement for TCP and UDP protocols
B. A more sophisticated form of encryption for data transmission
C. An upgrade path from RADIUS with more flexibility and capabilities

D. A replacement for physical access control mechanisms

450. What is the purpose of context-dependent access control?
A. To restrict access based on the user's job role
B. To make access decisions based on the sensitivity of the data
C. To make access decisions based on the collection of information
D. To filter content based on specific strings like "confidential."

451. How does a capability differ from an ACL in an access control matrix?
A. A capability corresponds to a column in the access control matrix, while an ACL corresponds to a row.
B. A capability is associated with the object, while an ACL is associated with the subject.
C. A capability corresponds to a row in the access control matrix, while an ACL corresponds to a column.
D. A capability is a physical token, while an ACL is a digital list.

452. Which protocol allows either end to initiate communication?

A. PAP
B. CHAP
C. Diameter
D. EAP

453. What does mobile IP technology allow a user to do?
A. Encrypt their data packets during mobile transfers
B. Use the same IP address even when moving from one network to another
C. Authenticate using biometrics on mobile devices
D. Access mobile networks at a reduced cost

454. What is the primary purpose of user access reviews?
A. To increase security measures periodically
B. To ensure no active accounts are unneeded or outdated

C. To check the performance of the IT department
D. To update the organization's access control policies

455. Which stakeholders are commonly engaged in the provisioning process of a user's digital identity?

A. Only the IT department
B. Human resources, the individual's supervisor, and the IT department
C. External consultants and the individual's colleagues
D. The individual alone

456. At what point in a user's association with an organization does provisioning normally occur?

A. At termination
B. During performance reviews
C. When a new user or system is added
D. On an annual basis

457. What is a potential challenge with de-provisioning accounts?
A. It can result in a security breach
B. It can leave behind orphaned resources
C. It can cause network congestion
D. It requires extra staffing

458. What is the importance of documenting why an account was provisioned?
A. To keep track of employee performance
B. For potential legal reasons
C. To determine whether the account should remain active or be de-provisioned later
D. To monitor the number of accounts created

459. What happens when an employee is terminated in relation to their user account?

A. Their access is expanded
B. Their account is usually deprovisioned
C. Their account is monitored for an additional year
D. Their account is handed over to another employee

460. Why are periodic system account access reviews necessary?
A. To comply with software licensing terms
B. To adjust system settings for optimal performance
C. To ensure no unnecessary or potentially privileged system accounts remain
D. To provide data for IT department audits

461. Which department is usually not involved in system account access reviews?

A. Information Technology (IT)
B. Research and Development (R&D)
C. Human Resources (HR)
D. Security Operations (SO)

462. What can trigger a user access review outside of the regular review schedule?

A. A successful software update
B. An extended leave of absence
C. A change in company leadership
D. An annual general meeting

463. What should be done when de-provisioning a user account to prevent operational hindrance?

A. Inform all employees about the deprovisioning
B. Transfer ownership of the user's resources to another individual
C. Archive the user's account for historical purposes
D. Encrypt all files associated with the user's account

464. What are the three broad categories of access control?

A. Administrative, Technical, and Physical
B. Operational, Managerial, and Environmental
C. Directive, Preventive and Detective
D. Organizational, Network, and Systemic

465. Which type of access control includes security awareness training?
A. Physical
B. Technical
C. Administrative
D. Operational

466. What is the primary role of physical controls in access control?

A. To encrypt data transmissions
B. To regulate logical access to systems
C. To support and work with administrative and technical controls
D. To monitor network traffic and detect intrusions

467. Which control would prevent a disgruntled employee from deleting financial statements?
A. Network architecture
B. Personnel controls
C. Perimeter security
D. Encryption and protocols

468. Which form of access control is primarily concerned with the flow of communication between network segments?

A. Network segregation
B. Supervisory structure
C. Cabling
D. System access

469. What is the function of technical controls in access control?
A. To enforce company policies and procedures
B. To physically secure the company's assets
C. To regulate logical access to systems and information
D. To provide security training to employees

470. What is the purpose of segregating a company's network into different zones?

A. To manage electrical interference between devices
B. To facilitate better communication between departments
C. To define different access controls based on the sensitivity of data
D. To distribute internet access evenly across the organization

471. What is the name given to the approach that uses both symmetric and asymmetric encryption methods together?
A. Session key method
B. Digital envelope
C. Key mixing
D. Public Key Infrastructure (PKI)

472. Which example best illustrates a supervisory structure as an administrative control?

A. A company uses fences around the building perimeter.
B. A manager is held accountable for their employee's actions.
C. A network is divided into subnets for logical segregation.
D. A firewall restricts access to a company's internal network.

473. Which cryptographic method provides authentication by ensuring a message is encrypted by a specific individual's private key?
A. Stream ciphers
B. Symmetric cryptography
C. Asymmetric cryptography

D. Block ciphers

474. What is the main purpose of implementing good access control practices in a network environment?

A. To increase the efficiency of the system
B. To make the user experience more personalized
C. To ensure security stays at a satisfactory level
D. To reduce the cost of the network infrastructure

475. Which of the following is not a recommended task for maintaining security in a network environment?

A. Removing obsolete user accounts immediately
B. Enforcing password rotation and requirements
C. Increasing the number of administrator accounts for redundancy
D. Denying access to systems to undefined users or anonymous accounts

476. What is object reuse in the context of information security?

A. Reusing code objects in software development
B. Assigning media that previously contained information to a new user
C. Reusing passwords across different accounts
D. Allowing users to reuse their old usernames

477. What should be done to previously used media before allowing someone to use it?

A. It should be labeled with the previous owner's name
B. It should be erased or degaussed
C. It should be physically destroyed
D. It should only be used by the same department

478. What does TEMPEST technology primarily aim to prevent?

A. Unauthorized physical access to devices
B. Cyber attacks like phishing and malware

C. Leakage of information through electrical signal emissions

D. Software piracy

479. What type of environments typically require the use of TEMPEST equipment?

A. Educational institutions

B. Commercial businesses

C. Military Institutions

D. Home offices

480. How does white noise serve as a countermeasure in information security?

A. It encrypts data transmissions

B. It adds random electrical signals to mask real information

C. It physically blocks signals from leaving a facility

D. It detects and alerts on unauthorized access attempts

481. What does a control zone in a facility do to enhance security?

A. It monitors internet traffic

B. It contains electrical signals with special material in the walls

C. It restricts user access based on job roles

D. It deploys guards at strategic locations

482. Which of the following algorithms is an example of an asymmetric key algorithm?

A. Advanced Encryption Standard (AES)

B. Data Encryption Standard (DES)

C. Digital Signature Algorithm (DSA)

D. Rivest Cipher 4 (RC4)

483. What should be done if media containing sensitive information cannot be purged?

A. It should be archived for future use
B. It should be used only by top management
C. It should be securely destroyed
D. It should be left untouched until data is overwritten

484. What is the main disadvantage of using symmetric cryptography when dealing with a large volume of users?
A. Speed of encryption
B. Difficulty in managing keys
C. Lack of confidentiality
D. Easier to break

485. Which type of IDS uses sensors to monitor network communications?
A. Host-Based IDS (HIDS)
B. Network-Based IDS (NIDS)
C. Application-Based IDS (AIDS)
D. Protocol Anomaly-Based IDS (PAIDS)

486. Which of the following is NOT a component of an IDS?
A. Sensors
B. Analyzers
C. Administrator interfaces
D. Encryption algorithms

487. Signature-based IDSs are unable to detect

A. Known attacks with existing signatures
B. Land attacks
C. Zero-day attacks
D. Attacks that match predefined patterns

488. A host-based IDS (HIDS) can be installed to monitor:
A. Individual workstations and servers
B. Network traffic

C. Electrical emissions from devices

D. Virtual private networks

489. Which type of IDS is capable of detecting new, unrecognized attacks by comparing activities to a learned profile of "normal" behavior?

A. Signature-based

B. State-based

C. Statistical anomaly-based

D. Rule-based

490. The term 'heuristic' in the context of IDS refers to?

A. The encryption of data

B. The creation of new information from different data sources

C. The physical security of devices

D. The use of safe listing techniques

491. How many symmetric keys are needed if 10 people need to communicate securely with each other?

A. 10

B. 45

C. 100

D. 50

492. What functionalities activate promiscuous mode on a Network Interface Card (NIC) and enable it to perform?

A. Encrypt all traffic passing through it

B. Capture all network traffic

C. Act as a firewall and block malicious packets

D. Perform heuristic analysis of network traffic

493. In a switched network environment, why might it be necessary to use a spanning port for an IDS?

A. To encrypt data with a stronger algorithm

B. To reduce the overhead on the IDS
C. To capture traffic from all virtual circuits
D. To act as a redundant system for the IDS

494. What is the primary goal of cryptography?

A. To create unreadable formats of data for everyone.
B. To transmit data in a readable format to anyone.
C. To protect data by encoding it so only authorized individuals can read it.
D. To make data transmission over networks slower and more secure.

495. What was the primary use of hieroglyphics in Egypt around 2000 B.C.?
A. As a complex encryption method to hide military secrets.
B. To decorate tombs with encrypted life stories of the deceased.
C. To make the life story of the deceased seem more noble and ceremonial.
D. As a way to communicate secret messages among the living.

496. What is the Atbash encryption scheme an example of?

A. Polyalphabetic substitution cipher
B. Transposition cipher
C. Monoalphabetic substitution cipher
D. Rotor cipher machine

497. What encryption method did Julius Caesar develop?

A. A polyalphabetic substitution cipher
B. A transposition cipher
C. A monoalphabetic substitution cipher with a shift of three positions
D. The first rotor cipher machine

498. What was the ROT13 encryption method used for in the 1980s?
A. To protect sensitive government information.
B. To encode inappropriate material in online forums.
C. To transmit encrypted military communications.

D. To create unbreakable codes for financial transactions.

499. Who developed a polyalphabetic substitution cipher for Henry III?

A. William Friedman
B. The Spartans
C. Blaise de Vigenère
D. Julius Caesar

500. Which device was a significant advancement in military cryptography during World War II?
A. The Atbash encryption scheme
B. The Vigenère cipher
C. The scytale cipher
D. The rotor cipher machine

501. Who is known as the "Father of Modern Cryptography"?
A. Blaise de Vigenère
B. William Frederick Friedman
C. Julius Caesar
D. Benedict Arnold

502. What was the U.S. Data Encryption Standard (DES) based on?
A. The Atbash encryption scheme
B. The Lucifer project developed at IBM
C. The Caesar cipher
D. The Vigenère cipher

503. What is cryptanalysis?
A. The study of creating strong encryption methods.
B. The science of studying and breaking the secrecy of encryption processes.
C. The practice of using cryptography in government applications.

D. The method of encrypting messages using hieroglyphics.

504. How does the complexity of the mathematics in today's symmetric algorithms affect their security against frequency-analysis attacks?
A. It has no effect; the attacks are still successful.
B. It slightly increases security, but not significantly.
C. It makes the encryption vulnerable to attacks.
D. It is too complex to allow for successful frequency-analysis attacks.

505. What does a cryptosystem consist of?
A. Software, protocols, algorithms, and keys
B. Encryption, decryption protocol, and digital signatures
C. Passwords, usernames, and access controls
D. Firewalls, antivirus software, and intrusion detection systems

506. What is Kerckhoff's Principle regarding cryptography?
A. The key should be the only secret element in a cryptosystem
B. Cryptography should rely on multiple secrets for security
C. Algorithms must remain secret for effective security
D. The longer the key, the less secure the cryptosystem

507. What is the purpose of a large keyspace in an encryption algorithm?
A. To make the encryption process faster
B. To reduce the computational requirements for encryption
C. To provide more possible values for the key, making it harder to guess
D. To decrease the size of the encrypted message

508. What is a one-time pad in cryptography?

A. A reusable encryption key
B. An encryption scheme that uses a single key for multiple messages
C. An encryption scheme that is considered unbreakable if used correctly
D. A pad used for secure hand-written messages

509. What are the requirements for a one-time pad to be unbreakable?
A. The pad must be pseudorandom and used multiple times
B. The pad must be short, predictable, and reused
C. The pad must be truly random, used once, and at least as long as the message
D. The pad must be digital and encrypted

510. Which aspect of the encryption process remains static in symmetric algorithms?

A. The key material
B. The encryption speed
C. The algorithm
D. The key generation process

511. Which of the following is an example of a running key cipher?
A. A cipher that uses a book page and line number as its key
B. A cipher that only runs on a specific type of computer system
C. A cipher that continuously changes its keys during communication
D. A cipher that runs at a very high speed for quick encryption

512. What is the Least Significant bit (LSB) method in steganography?
A. A technique for encrypting messages with the lowest possible security
B. A method of embedding secret data by altering the least significant bits of a file
C. A method for creating the smallest possible file size for encryption
D. A technique for reducing the bit rate of an audio file for easier transmission

513. What are subkeys in the context of key derivation?
A. Keys that are less secure than the master key.
B. The only keys used in symmetric encryption.
C. Keys created from a master key.
D. Keys that are used for public-key cryptography.

514. What are the two basic types of ciphers used in symmetric encryption algorithms?
A. Asymmetric and symmetric
B. Substitution and transposition
C. Block and stream
D. Public and private

515. In a substitution cipher, what determines how the substitution is carried out?

A. The algorithm
B. The key
C. The prime numbers
D. The public and private key pair

516. Which letter replacement would the Caesar cipher used to encrypt the letter 'm' if the key is to shift three places?
A. p
B. o
C. n
D. q

517. What is the role of a key in a transposition cipher?

A. It replaces the characters with other characters.
B. It dictates the positions to which the values are moved.
C. It remains constant throughout the encryption process.
D. It determines the length of the message.

518. What is the main reason for using different keys to encrypt different messages?
A. To maintain the same level of complexity for each message.
B. To add randomness and secrecy to the encryption process.
C. To comply with international encryption standards.

D. To make the encryption process simpler.

519. What is the potential vulnerability of simple substitution and transposition ciphers?
A. They are too slow to be practical.
B. They cannot be used on digital systems.
C. They are susceptible to frequency-analysis attacks.
D. They require too much keying material to be secure.

520. What is the purpose of Key Derivation Functions (KDFs)?
A. To weaken the encryption for faster decryption.
B. To generate keys with random values.
C. To create public keys for asymmetric encryption.
D. To simplify the encryption algorithm.

521. Which of the following best describes the principle of least privilege?

A. Users are granted access to all systems by default.

B. Users are given only the access necessary to perform their job functions.

C. Access rights are granted based on user requests.

D. Users have access to the most critical systems and data.

522. What is the primary purpose of data classification?

A. To enforce encryption policies

B. To determine the value and sensitivity of data

C. To create a backup schedule

D. To limit access to physical assets

523. Which type of access control model grants permissions based on predefined roles within an organization?

A. Discretionary Access Control (DAC)

B. Mandatory Access Control (MAC)

C. Role-Based Access Control (RBAC)

D. Attribute-Based Access Control (ABAC)


524. Which protocol is commonly used to secure email communications?

A. HTTP

B. SMTP

C. IMAP

D. S/MIME


525. What is the primary purpose of single sign-on (SSO)?

A. To enforce multifactor authentication

B. To allow users to access multiple applications with one set of credentials

C. To provide biometric authentication

D. To implement session management


526. Which testing method involves evaluating the security of a system by simulating an attack from a malicious source?

A. Vulnerability assessment

B. Penetration testing

C. Code review

D. Security audit


527. What is the primary goal of incident response?

A. To perform regular security audits

B. To recover from security breaches and minimize damage

C. To implement security policies

D. To train employees on security awareness

528. Which practice involves reviewing the source code of an application to identify and fix security vulnerabilities?

A. Fuzz testing

B. Black-box testing

C. Code review

D. Patch management

529. What security principle ensures that information is not disclosed to unauthorized individuals or entities?

A. Availability

B. Integrity

C. Confidentiality

D. Non-repudiation

530. Which legislation requires organizations to protect the privacy and security of personal health information (PHI) in the United States?

A. GDPR (General Data Protection Regulation)

B. HIPAA (Health Insurance Portability and Accountability Act)

C. CCPA (California Consumer Privacy Act)

D. FISMA (Federal Information Security Management Act)

531. Which of the following is a key characteristic of a quantitative risk assessment?

A. Subjective analysis based on expert judgment

B. Use of statistical techniques and data to quantify risks

C. Assessment of risks using predefined scales like high, medium, and low

D. Focus on identifying vulnerabilities and threats

532. In the context of asset management, what is the purpose of a hardware asset management (HAM) system?

A. To track software licenses and usage

B. To manage physical assets like servers and networking equipment

C. To monitor and control access to sensitive data

D. To enforce encryption policies on hardware devices

533. Which cryptographic algorithm is commonly used for both encryption and digital signatures in secure communications?

A. RSA

B. AES

C. SHA-256

D. Diffie-Hellman

534. Which network security protocol operates at the Application Layer of the OSI model and provides secure remote login and file transfer capabilities?

A. IPsec

B. SSL/TLS

C. SSH

D. PPTP

535. Which authentication factor is considered the strongest for verifying a user's identity?

A. Something the user knows (password)

B. Something the user has (smart card)

C. Something the user is (biometric)

D. Something the user does (behavioral)

536. What is the primary goal of dynamic application security testing (DAST)?

A. To analyze the source code of an application for vulnerabilities

B. To simulate attacks against an application in real-time

C. To identify security weaknesses by analyzing application behavior

D. To verify the functionality and usability of an application

537. Which of the following is a key component of a security incident response plan?

A. Routine vulnerability scans

B. Business impact analysis (BIA)

C. Chain of custody procedures

D. Change management controls

538. Which software development methodology emphasizes collaboration between cross-functional teams and iterative development cycles?

A. Waterfall model

B. Agile methodology

C. Spiral model

D. RAD (Rapid Application Development)

539. What security principle ensures that data cannot be modified or tampered with by unauthorized individuals?

A. Integrity

B. Availability

C. Confidentiality

D. Non-repudiation


540. Which regulation requires organizations to implement measures to protect personal data and privacy of individuals within the European Union?

A. HIPAA

B. CCPA

C. GDPR

D. FISMA


541. Which risk assessment methodology evaluates risks based on their potential impact on an organization's mission-critical operations and objectives?

A. Quantitative risk analysis

B. Business impact analysis (BIA)

C. Delphi technique

D. Fault tree analysis


542. In the context of software asset management (SAM), what is the purpose of a software license management system?

A. To track software installations across network devices

B. To manage software vendors' contracts and agreements

C. To optimize software license usage and compliance

D. To enforce software update policies

543. Which cryptographic protocol is designed to provide secure key exchange between parties over an insecure communication channel?

A. Diffie-Hellman

B. RSA

C. AES

D. HMAC

544. Which security protocol is primarily used to protect web traffic by providing confidentiality, integrity, and authentication?

A. TLS (Transport Layer Security)

B. IPsec (Internet Protocol Security)

C. SSL (Secure Sockets Layer)

D. SSH (Secure Shell)

545. What is the primary purpose of a federated identity management system in a multi-organization environment?

A. To synchronize user credentials across different organizations

B. To enable seamless access to shared resources using a single set of credentials

C. To enforce role-based access control (RBAC) policies across all organizations

D. To facilitate cross-domain trust relationships and authentication

546. What is the main objective of static application security testing (SAST)?

A. To identify security vulnerabilities by analyzing application behavior in real-time

B. To assess the security posture of an application without executing the code

C. To simulate attacks against an application to identify exploitable weaknesses

D. To verify the functionality and usability of an application under normal conditions

547. Which component of a disaster recovery plan (DRP) outlines the procedures for restoring critical business functions after a disruptive event?

A. Business continuity plan (BCP)

B. Backup and recovery plan

C. Emergency response plan

D. Crisis communication plan

548. Which software development model focuses on continuous integration and delivery (CI/CD), automated testing, and frequent code deployments?

A. Waterfall model

B. Spiral model

C. DevOps model

D. RAD (Rapid Application Development) model

549. What security principle ensures that actions or events cannot be denied or refuted by a party involved?

A. Integrity

B. Non-repudiation

C. Availability

D. Confidentiality

550. Which regulatory framework requires financial institutions to implement security measures to protect customer information and ensure the confidentiality and integrity of financial transactions?

A. GLBA (Gramm-Leach-Bliley Act)

B. SOX (Sarbanes-Oxley Act)

C. PCI DSS (Payment Card Industry Data Security Standard)

D. FERPA (Family Educational Rights and Privacy Act)

551. Which of the following is an essential component of a security governance framework?

A. Incident response procedures

B. Access control policies

C. Risk appetite statement

D. Network security protocols

552. In the context of information classification, what does the term "compartmentalization" refer to?

A. Restricting access to information based on sensitivity levels

B. Organizing information into distinct categories or groups

C. Encrypting data during transmission and storage

D. Applying digital watermarks to sensitive documents

553. Which security model emphasizes the hierarchical classification of information and enforces strict access control based on clearance levels?

A. Biba model

B. Clark-Wilson model

C. Bell-LaPadula model

D. Brewer-Nash model

554. What is the primary purpose of a network intrusion detection system (NIDS)?

A. To prevent unauthorized access to network resources

B. To detect and respond to suspicious network activities in real-time

C. To encrypt network traffic between endpoints

D. To monitor network bandwidth usage

555. Which access control mechanism dynamically adjusts user access privileges based on changes in user roles or responsibilities?

A. Rule-based access control (RBAC)

B. Attribute-based access control (ABAC)

C. Role-based access control (RBAC)

D. Mandatory access control (MAC)

556. What is the main objective of a black-box penetration test?

A. To analyze source code for vulnerabilities

B. To simulate an attack from an insider threat

C. To assess the effectiveness of security controls without prior knowledge of the system

D. To evaluate the resilience of critical infrastructure against cyber threats

557. Which metric is used to measure the effectiveness of a security incident response team?

A. Mean Time Between Failures (MTBF)

B. Mean Time to Detect (MTTD)

C. Mean Time to Respond (MTTR)

D. Recovery Point Objective (RPO)

558. Which software security testing technique involves manipulating input data to trigger unexpected behavior in an application?

A. Fuzz testing

B. Code review

C. Regression testing

D. Static analysis

559. What security principle ensures that information is available and accessible to authorized users when needed?

A. Integrity

B. Availability

C. Confidentiality

D. Non-repudiation

560. Which regulation mandates the implementation of controls to protect personal data processed within the European Union, regardless of where the processing takes place?

A. HIPAA (Health Insurance Portability and Accountability Act)

B. GLBA (Gramm-Leach-Bliley Act)

C. GDPR (General Data Protection Regulation)

D. FERPA (Family Educational Rights and Privacy Act)

# Answers

**1. Answer: A**

**Explanation:** The principle of least privilege is a fundamental security principle that dictates users should only have the minimum permissions required to perform their tasks. This minimizes the potential damage if a user account is compromised.

**2. Answer: A**

**Explanation:** While BCDR is a critical security concept, it is not explicitly covered in the CISSP CBK. The CISSP focuses on information security, and BCDR encompasses a broader range of business continuity considerations.

**3. Answer: A**

**Explanation:** Preventive controls are designed to stop security incidents from happening. Examples include access controls, firewalls, and intrusion detection systems.

**4. Answer: D**

**Explanation:** An MitM attack intercepts communication between two parties, allowing the attacker to steal data or impersonate one of the parties.

**5. Answer: C**

**Explanation:** Strong and unique passwords are essential for preventing unauthorized access. Users should avoid using the same password for multiple accounts and refrain from sharing passwords with others.

**6. Answer: B**

**Explanation:** Penetration testing is a controlled process where authorized experts simulate cyber attacks on a system to uncover vulnerabilities. By exploiting these weaknesses, they help organizations identify and fix security issues before malicious hackers can exploit them. This proactive approach strengthens the overall security posture of the system or network.

**7. Answer: B**

**Explanation:** Asymmetric encryption involves two keys: a public key, which encrypts data, and a private key, which decrypts it. Data encrypted with the public key can only be decrypted with the corresponding private key, ensuring secure communication.

8. **Answer:** B

**Explanation:** SIEM systems aggregate security logs from different devices and applications, allowing for centralized monitoring and analysis of security events.

9. **Answer:** A

**Explanation:** Phishing attacks attempt to trick users into revealing sensitive information or clicking malicious links by posing as legitimate entities.

10. **Answer:** B

**Explanation:** The CIA triad represents the three core security objectives: confidentiality (ensuring data privacy), integrity (maintaining data accuracy and completeness), and availability (ensuring authorized access to data).

11. **Answer:** B

**Explanation:** Risk management aims to identify, assess, and mitigate risks to an acceptable level rather than eliminating all risks. This approach recognizes that complete risk elimination is often impractical or impossible, and attempting to do so could be overly costly or disruptive. Instead, the focus is on managing risks effectively to ensure they are within acceptable thresholds while enabling the organization to pursue its objectives efficiently.

12. **Answer:** B

**Explanation:** This classification system categorizes data based on its sensitivity and importance, guiding organizations in implementing suitable security measures, access restrictions, and protective measures tailored to each category's needs.

13. **Answer:** B

**Explanation:** Firewalls are security barriers that monitor and control network traffic based on predefined rules, safeguarding networks from unauthorized access and cyber threats. They examine data packets and decide whether to allow or block them based on factors like source/destination addresses, ports, and protocols.

## 14. Answer: C

**Explanation:** SMTP is commonly used for email communications. While it doesn't inherently provide security, extensions like STARTTLS can be used for encryption. Additionally, other email security protocols like SPF, DKIM, and DMARC are often implemented alongside SMTP to enhance security.

## 15. Answer: C

**Explanation:** Natural territorial reinforcement creates physical designs that emphasize or extend an organization's sphere of influence, making legitimate users feel a sense of ownership while signaling to potential offenders that their illicit activities will be noticed and not tolerated.

## 16. Answer: A

**Explanation:** Penetration testing is conducted to identify vulnerabilities in a system by simulating real-world attacks.

## 17. Answer: B

**Explanation:** The incident response plan is a structured approach to handling security incidents. It includes preparation, identification, containment, eradication, recovery, lessons learned, and communication/reporting. Its goal is to minimize the impact of incidents and facilitate a coordinated response to restore normal operations quickly.

## 18. Answer: C

**Explanation:** Integrating security into the SDLC helps identify and address security issues at an early stage, reducing the risk of vulnerabilities in the final product.

## 19. Answer: B

**Explanation:** A security policy is a documented set of rules, guidelines, and procedures established by an organization to protect its information assets and resources, which outlines

## 20. Answer: B

**Explanation:** Physical security controls are measures put in place to protect assets, facilities, and personnel from environmental hazards, theft, vandalism, and other physical risks. They include systems like locks, access control, surveillance cameras, and emergency response procedures to prevent unauthorized access and mitigate potential threats.

**21. Answer: B**

**Explanation:** SoD minimizes the risk of unauthorized activity by ensuring that no single user has all the permissions necessary to complete a sensitive task. This helps to enhance accountability, detect and deter fraud, and safeguard against insider threats.

**22. Answer: B**

**Explanation:** The DMZ allows organizations to offer public services (e.g., web servers) while adding an extra layer of security between the public internet and the internal network.

**23. Answer: B**

**Explanation:** Symmetric encryption uses the same key for both encryption and decryption, making it efficient for bulk data encryption.

**24. Answer: D**

**Explanation:** ISO 27001 is a globally recognized standard that outlines best practices for implementing an ISMS.

**25. Answer: B**

**Explanation:** Vulnerability scanning uses automated tools to detect weaknesses in systems and applications. It categorizes scans based on scope, conducts scheduled or on-demand assessments, prioritizes risks, meets compliance requirements, integrates with other security measures, and requires continuous improvement to stay effective against evolving threats.

**26. Answer: B**

**Explanation:** The main reason for conducting a risk analysis in the site planning process is to identify the organization's vulnerabilities, threats, and business impacts. This analysis is crucial for defining an acceptable risk level for the physical security program and developing effective countermeasures.

**27. Answer: B**

**Explanation:** MFA adds an extra layer of security by requiring something you know (password), something you have (token), or something you are (biometric) for authentication.

**28. Answer: B**

**Explanation:** When storing data in the cloud, organizations entrust the physical security of their data to the cloud provider, which implements stringent measures, including access controls, surveillance, and certifications. While organizations relinquish direct control over the physical environment, they can ensure security through shared responsibility models, risk assessments, and transparency mechanisms provided by the cloud provider.

**29. Answer: B**

**Explanation:** A Business Continuity Plan (BCP) outlines how an organization will recover critical operations following a disruptive event. It identifies critical functions, assesses risks, develops recovery strategies, specifies response procedures, allocates resources, conducts testing and training, and maintains documentation for ongoing review and updates.

**30. Answer: C**

**Explanation:** A MitM attack aims to intercept communication, while DoS attacks focus on overwhelming a system with traffic to render it unavailable to legitimate users.

**31. Answer: C**

**Explanation:** Information security governance ensures that an organization's security efforts protect its information assets while supporting its business goals. This involves aligning security with business objectives, managing risks, complying with regulations, engaging stakeholders, and continuously improving security practices.

**32. Answer: B**

**Explanation:** Smoke detectors should be installed above suspended ceilings and below raised floors, as well as in air vents, to ensure early detection of fire. These areas are common places for wires and electrical equipment that could potentially start a fire, and early detection is crucial for a timely response.

## 33. Answer: A

**Explanation:** Security architecture is all about creating and setting up systems and structures in a way that keeps them safe from threats or attacks. It involves designing and building frameworks that prioritize security, making sure that sensitive information and resources are protected from unauthorized access or malicious activities.

## 34. Answer: D

**Explanation:** WPA3 is a type of security technology that helps keep Wi-Fi networks safe from unauthorized access. It's a protocol that sets standards for how devices connect to and communicate over wireless networks, adding layers of protection to prevent hackers or other intruders from getting into the network without permission.

## 35. Answer: B

**Explanation:** CPTED is a discipline that outlines how the proper design of a physical environment can reduce crime by directly affecting human behavior. It aims to create behavioral effects that will reduce crime and the fear of crime through strategic environmental design.

## 36. Answer: B

**Explanation:** A vulnerability assessment is a process that looks for and measures weaknesses in a system or network. Its goal is to find and understand any potential security flaws that attackers could exploit. By identifying these vulnerabilities, organizations can prioritize and take steps to fix them, making their systems and networks more secure.

## 37. Answer: C

**Explanation:** Pre-action systems are similar to dry pipe systems, where the water is not stored in the pipes. They allow for a delay after the initial fire detection before water is released, giving time to address false alarms or small fires that can be managed without the sprinkler system, thus avoiding unnecessary water damage to sensitive electronic equipment.

## 38. Answer: B

**Explanation:** Verifying the effectiveness of security controls during a security audit helps assess whether systems and processes comply with established security policies and standards.

### 39. Answer: C

**Explanation:** Business Impact Analysis (BIA) is a method used to pinpoint and rank essential business operations and their interconnections to ensure efficient risk management. It helps organizations understand which processes are most crucial to their operations and how they rely on each other. By identifying these critical processes and dependencies, businesses can better prepare for and mitigate potential risks, ensuring continuity even in the face of disruptions or disasters.

### 40. Answer: D

**Explanation:** Hardware Security Modules (HSMs) are special-purpose devices created to safeguard and oversee cryptographic keys. These keys are used for encryption, decryption, and authentication in various security protocols and applications. HSMs provide a highly secure environment for generating, storing, and managing these keys, ensuring they remain protected from unauthorized access or tampering. They play a crucial role in enhancing the security of sensitive data and transactions in various industries, such as finance, healthcare, and government.

### 41. Answer: B

**Explanation:** The CISSP emphasizes the importance of building security into software from the beginning (secure coding practices, threat modeling) throughout the development process.

### 42. Answer: B

**Explanation:** Phishing emails attempt to trick recipients into clicking malicious links or revealing sensitive information by impersonating legitimate entities (e.g., banks).

### 43. Answer: B

**Explanation:** Security Operations Centers (SOCs) serve as central hubs for ongoing security monitoring, analysis of system logs, and detection of potential security incidents. Essentially, SOCs are dedicated facilities or teams responsible for actively monitoring and defending an organization's IT infrastructure against cyber threats. They continuously monitor network traffic, system logs, and other security data sources to identify suspicious activities or anomalies that could indicate a security breach. Once identified, these potential security incidents are investigated further, and appropriate response measures are taken to mitigate the threat and protect the organization's assets and data.

### 44. Answer: C

**Explanation:** Personally Identifiable Information (PII) refers to any data that can be used to identify a specific individual, such as name, address, Social Security number, etc.

### 45. Answer: B

**Explanation:** Detective controls are designed to identify security incidents after they have occurred, such as Intrusion Detection Systems (IDS) and Security Information and Event Management (SIEM) systems.

### 46. Answer: C

**Explanation:** Encryption at rest scrambles data on storage devices, making it unreadable if accessed by unauthorized individuals.

### 47. Answer: B

**Explanation:** A vulnerability is a weakness in a system that can be exploited. A threat is an actor or event that can potentially exploit a vulnerability to cause harm.

### 48. Answer: C

**Explanation:** Creating strong passwords involves using a combination of different character types, such as uppercase and lowercase letters, numbers, and symbols. This makes the password more complex and harder for attackers to guess through brute-force methods. Additionally, avoiding easily guessable information such as personal details (like birthdays or pet names) and avoiding password reuse across multiple accounts are also essential best practices for maintaining strong password security.

### 49. Answer: B

**Explanation:** Defense in depth is a strategy for enhancing security by implementing multiple layers of protection and controls. Instead of relying solely on a single security measure, this approach uses a combination of defenses at various points throughout an organization's IT infrastructure. By layering these defenses, such as firewalls, intrusion detection systems, encryption, access controls, and security policies, it becomes more challenging for attackers to breach the system.

**50. Answer: C**

**Explanation:** Mantraps are small rooms with two doors designed to control access to secure areas. They are used to prevent piggybacking by trapping an individual between two sets of doors until they are authenticated, ensuring that only authorized personnel gain access to sensitive areas.

**51. Answer: D**

**Explanation:** The Chief Information Security Officer (CISO) is in charge of supervising and administering the organization's information security efforts.

**52. Answer: B**

**Explanation:** An Information Asset Inventory systematically catalogs and organizes all data resources held by an organization, facilitating effective management, categorization, and safeguarding of sensitive information.

**53. Answer: B**

**Explanation:** The Bell-LaPadula Model prioritizes the protection of data confidentiality, integrity, and availability, forming the basis for secure access control policies in information systems. It emphasizes restricting access to information based on security classifications and enforcing rules to prevent unauthorized data disclosure or modification, ensuring the data remains secure and accessible to authorized users.

**54. Answer: B**

**Explanation:** VPNs encrypt data for secure transmission over untrusted networks, enhancing confidentiality and integrity.

**55. Answer: C**

**Explanation:** When considering physical security, professionals are concerned with how people can physically enter an environment and the potential damage they can cause, which differs from the focus on technology-oriented security breaches in information security.

**56. Answer: B**

**Explanation:** Supply system threats are related to the disruptions in the utilities and services that an organization relies on to operate. Power distribution outages specifically refer to interruptions in the electrical power supply, which can severely impact an organization's ability to function. These outages can affect data centers, communication systems, and other critical infrastructure, making them a significant supply system threat.

**57. Answer: D**

**Explanation:** A good security plan should consider a broad range of threats, including natural environmental threats, supply system threats, manufactured threats, and politically motivated threats.

**58. Answer: D**

**Explanation:** The primary goal of good security practices in an organization is to create a secure and predictable environment. This ensures that the organization's assets, including information, physical infrastructure, and personnel, are protected from threats. A secure environment allows employees to focus on their tasks without worrying about security issues, supports business continuity, and enhances trust and confidence among stakeholders. The other options reflect negative or counterproductive outcomes that are not aligned with the objectives of good security practices.

**59. Answer: C**

**Explanation:** A Privacy Impact Assessment evaluates potential privacy risks in a project or system by identifying and analyzing how personal data is collected, used, and protected. It helps organizations ensure compliance with privacy regulations and implement measures to mitigate risks and protect individuals' privacy.

**60 Answer: C**

**Explanation:** Key escrow entails securely storing cryptographic keys with a trusted third party for potential recovery if the keys are lost. This backup measure ensures continuity and access to encrypted data, enhancing security.

### 61. Answer: C

**Explanation:** CISSP emphasizes one-way hashing algorithms (e.g., bcrypt, SHA-256) with a random salt to protect password security. The salt makes it computationally infeasible to derive the original password from the hash.

### 62. Answer: B

**Explanation:** Input validation and sanitization involve checking user input for malicious code before processing it. This helps prevent SQL injection attacks where attackers inject malicious SQL code into website forms.

### 63. Answer: C

**Explanation:** Natural disasters are under natural environmental threats, not under manufactured threats. Manufactured threats include unauthorized access, damage by disgruntled employees, employee errors and accidents, vandalism, fraud, theft, and others.

### 64. Answer: B

**Explanation:** Digital certificates issued by trusted authorities verify the identity of servers and clients involved in communication, establishing trust and preventing man-in-the-middle attacks.

### 65. Answer: C

**Explanation:** Using a layered defense model to balance life safety concerns with security measures.

### 66. Answer: B

**Explanation:** Testing the BCDR plan identifies potential weaknesses and ensures a smooth recovery process in case of a disaster. Backups should be stored off-site to safeguard data from physical incidents.

### 67. Answer: C

**Explanation:** The primary consideration is life safety. Protecting human life is the priority, and it should take precedence over all other types of security measures.

**68. Answer: B**

**Explanation:** Worms are malicious software capable of autonomously duplicating and spreading through networks. They exploit vulnerabilities to infect susceptible devices, propagating rapidly without user intervention. Worms pose significant cybersecurity threats, as they can disrupt networks, steal data, and deploy additional malicious payloads. Implementing robust security measures and promptly patching vulnerabilities are crucial for mitigating worm-related risks.

**69. Answer: B**

**Explanation:** SA&A involves a systematic evaluation of security controls to determine if they are adequate and functioning correctly to meet organizational security needs.

**70. Answer: A**

**Explanation:** Web filtering blocks access to phishing websites, safeguarding users from clicking on malicious links or downloading harmful content. This proactive security measure helps prevent potential cyber threats and protects sensitive data from being compromised. By filtering out suspicious URLs and content, organizations can bolster their defenses against phishing attacks and mitigate the risk of malware infections.

**71. Answer: B**

**Explanation:** Network segmentation creates logical barriers within a network, restricting traffic flow and potentially containing security incidents within a specific segment.

**72. Answer: B**

**Explanation:** Defining user access controls and permissions in the cloud application is crucial to ensure that only authorized users can access sensitive data.

**73. Answer: B**

**Explanation:** Algebraic attacks specifically target the vulnerabilities in the mathematics of an algorithm, exploiting its intrinsic algebraic structure. These attacks analyze the algorithm's functions and attempt to find weaknesses that can be used to break the encryption.

## 74. Answer: D

**Explanation:** Post-Quantum Cryptography (PQC) refers to cryptographic algorithms designed to be secure against attacks by quantum computers, unlike traditional algorithms like RSA and ECC, which are vulnerable to quantum attacks.

## 75. Answer: B

**Explanation:** MDM solutions enforce security policies on mobile devices, including strong passwords, remote wipe capabilities, and application restrictions, to protect sensitive data.

## 76. Answer: B

**Explanation:** Replay attacks entail retransmitting intercepted data to trick a system into accepting it as genuine. Timestamps and sequence numbers are employed to counter such attacks. Packets are timestamped and expected within a designated timeframe, while unique sequence numbers prevent the replay of outdated data.

## 77. Answer: C

**Explanation:** DoS attacks aim to overwhelm a system with traffic, making it unavailable to legitimate users. Analyzing the attack pattern and implementing mitigation strategies (e.g., traffic filtering and DDoS protection services) are crucial for restoring service.

## 78. Answer: C

**Explanation:** A risk assessment is conducted to identify, evaluate, and prioritize risks, enabling informed decision-making on risk mitigation.

## 79. Answer: C

**Explanation:** Side-channel attacks do not directly attack the mathematical basis of the cryptosystem. Instead, they gather external information, such as power consumption, radiation emissions, and processing time, to infer the value of an encryption key.

**80. Answer: B**

**Explanation:** Stateful firewalls monitor the progress of network connections, maintaining awareness of their states, such as established, related, or new. Using this contextual understanding, they enforce security policies, allowing or blocking traffic based on predefined rules. By dynamically inspecting traffic, stateful firewalls enhance network security by distinguishing legitimate communication from potentially malicious activity, thereby fortifying defenses against cyber threats.

**81. Answer: B**

**Explanation:** Remote Authentication Dial-In User Service (RADIUS) is a protocol used for authenticating and authorizing remote users attempting to access a network. It provides a centralized authentication server where user credentials are verified before granting access. RADIUS offers a secure and efficient way to manage remote user access across various network devices and services. This protocol is widely utilized in enterprises, ISPs, and telecommunications networks for secure remote authentication and access control.

**82. Answer: B**

**Explanation:** Security audits assess the efficiency of security measures and protocols put in place within an organization. They examine whether implemented controls and policies align with industry standards and regulatory requirements. By identifying vulnerabilities and areas for improvement, security audits help enhance overall security posture and mitigate potential risks. Organizations conduct security audits regularly to ensure continuous monitoring and improvement of their security measures.

**83. Answer: C**

**Explanation:** Public algorithms are known and can be scrutinized by the public, allowing for peer review and improvements based on collective expertise. On the other hand, secret algorithms are not released to the public for examination, as is the case with those developed by the NSA.

**84. Answer: C**

**Explanation:** Input validation checks and cleanses user-provided data to thwart injection attacks, such as SQL injection or cross-site scripting. It ensures that input adheres to expected formats, rejecting any potentially malicious or unexpected content. By validating and sanitizing input, organizations can fortify their systems against exploitation, preserving data integrity and security.

**85. Answer: C**

**Explanation:** A Business Continuity Plan (BCP) prioritizes maintaining essential business operations amidst disruptions or disasters. It outlines strategies and procedures to sustain critical functions, minimize downtime, and facilitate rapid recovery. By preparing for various scenarios, including natural disasters or cyber incidents, BCPs enable organizations to mitigate risks and ensure continuity of operations. Regular testing and updates are essential to ensure effectiveness and readiness in times of crisis.

**86. Answer: B**

**Explanation:** Differential cryptanalysis, which analyzes ciphertext pairs generated by encryption of plaintext pairs with specific differences, was invented in 1990 and turned out to be an effective and successful attack against block algorithms like the Data Encryption Standard (DES).

**87. Answer: B**

**Explanation:** A well-tested and up-to-date disaster recovery plan is critical for a swift and effective response to minimize downtime and ensure business continuity.

**88. Answer: C**

**Explanation:** Unknown USB drives and files can harbor malware, posing a significant security threat to systems. To mitigate risks, it's safest to refrain from accessing the files and securely delete the USB drive. This precaution helps prevent potential infections and safeguard sensitive data from compromise. Vigilance and adherence to security best practices are crucial for maintaining a secure computing environment.

**89. Answer: B**

**Explanation:** Steganography involves concealing secret information within an ordinary, non-secret file or message in such a way that it does not attract attention to its existence.

### 90. Answer: B

**Explanation:** PCI DSS sets forth regulations for entities handling credit card information to ensure secure transactions. It mandates adherence to specific security measures and controls to protect cardholder data. Organizations storing, processing, or transmitting credit card data must comply with these requirements to prevent breaches and protect sensitive financial information. Compliance helps mitigate risks, builds trust with customers, and avoids penalties for non-compliance.

### 91. Answer: B

**Explanation:** Honeypots are dummy systems designed to mimic real targets, enticing attackers to engage with them. Security teams closely monitor these decoys to gather insights into attacker tactics, tools, and methods. By observing interactions with honeypots, organizations can improve their understanding of threats and strengthen overall cybersecurity defenses. Honeypots serve as valuable tools for detecting and studying malicious activities while minimizing risks to production systems.

### 92. Answer: B

**Explanation:** MFA makes things more secure by asking for multiple types of proof to confirm your identity. This could be something like a password (something you know), a token (something you have), or a biometric feature like a fingerprint (something you are). Fingerprint scanners are a type of biometric authentication that can be used to verify identity.

### 93. Answer: A

**Explanation:** Preventive controls aim to stop security incidents from happening in the first place. Restricting access to social media helps prevent potential security risks and wasted productivity.

### 94. Answer: B

**Explanation:** A centralized logging system allows for easier collection, analysis, and correlation of security events from various sources, enabling faster detection and response to potential threats.

## 95. Answer: C

**Explanation:** The CIA triad consists of three essential components: Confidentiality, Integrity, and Availability. Availability ensures that authorized users can access information and systems whenever necessary, maintaining uninterrupted operations and productivity. This aspect focuses on ensuring that resources are reliably accessible to legitimate users, minimizing downtime, and enabling timely access to critical data and services.

## 96. Answer: A

**Explanation:** Adaptive attacks are a derivative form of standard attacks, with the key difference being that the attacker can modify their strategy based on the information gleaned from the initial attack. This helps the attacker refine their approach to be more effective in subsequent attempts.

## 97. Answer: A

**Explanation:** Data encryption protects sensitive information at rest (stored in the cloud). And in transit (during transfer). This ensures unauthorized access even if data is intercepted.

## 98. Answer: C

**Explanation:** DoS attacks aim to flood a system with traffic, making it inaccessible for legitimate users. Attackers don't directly steal data or exploit vulnerabilities.

## 99. Answer: C

**Explanation:** In a chosen-ciphertext attack, the attacker's goal is to figure out the encryption key by choosing ciphertexts that can be decrypted and then gaining access to the resulting plaintext.

## 100. Answer: B

**Explanation:** In a chosen-plaintext attack, the attacker can choose the plaintext that gets encrypted. This allows the attacker to obtain the corresponding ciphertext, providing a deeper understanding of the encryption process and more information about the key being used.

**101. Answer: B**

**Explanation:** In a known-plaintext attack, the attacker has access to both the plaintext and the corresponding ciphertext. The goal is to discover the key used to encrypt the messages to decipher other messages encrypted with the same key.

**102. Answer: B**

**Explanation:** Endpoint Detection and Response (EDR) systems continuously monitor endpoints (user devices) for suspicious activity and malware infections, allowing for detection, investigation, and potential remediation.

**103. Answer: C**

**Explanation:** A ciphertext-only attack involves an attacker who has access to the ciphertext of multiple messages, all encrypted with the same algorithm, and attempts to discover the encryption key used. This attack is prevalent due to the ease of intercepting ciphertext traffic, yet it is challenging to succeed in because of limited information about the encryption process.

**104. Answer: B**

**Explanation:** CISSP emphasizes the importance of encryption (e.g., Using AES, TLS) to safeguard data confidentiality during communication, preventing unauthorized parties from reading the information.

**105. Answer: B**

**Explanation:** Pretexting involves creating a false scenario (e.g., IT support) to gain a user's trust and trick them into granting access or revealing sensitive information.

**106. Answer: B**

**Explanation:** Network segmentation partitions the network into logical zones, restricting traffic flow between them. This helps contain a security incident within a specific segment, minimizing potential damage.

## 107. Answer: B

**Explanation:** Secure SDLC emphasizes integrating security considerations throughout the development process (coding practices, threat modeling, security testing) to build security into the application from the ground up.

## 108. Answer: B

**Explanation:** DRM technologies regulate access to copyrighted content, dictating how it can be utilized, duplicated, and shared. They enforce restrictions to prevent unauthorized copying, distribution, or modification of digital assets. DRM mechanisms are employed to safeguard intellectual property rights and manage the distribution of digital media, ensuring compliance with licensing agreements and protecting content creators' interests. These technologies play a crucial role in maintaining control over digital content and preventing piracy.

## 109. Answer: B

**Explanation:** Sending keys without encryption is insecure; it's crucial to transmit and store them securely. Encryption ensures confidentiality, preventing unauthorized access to sensitive information. Secure transmission and storage protocols protect against interception and unauthorized use of keys, safeguarding the integrity and security of cryptographic systems. Adhering to secure practices mitigates the risk of unauthorized access and enhances overall security posture.

## 110. Answer: B

**Explanation:** The Key Distribution Center (KDC) is a core element of the Kerberos authentication protocol. It handles the automated distribution and management of cryptographic keys for secure communication. By facilitating seamless key exchange between users and services, the KDC streamlines authentication processes within a Kerberos realm, enhancing system security. This centralized approach simplifies key management and strengthens overall security infrastructure.

## 111. Answer: C

**Explanation:** The CIA triad comprises Confidentiality, Integrity, and Availability. Integrity ensures that data remains accurate and complete and cannot be altered without authorization.

## 112. Answer: D

**Explanation:** Non-repudiation guarantees that a message sender cannot disavow sending the message afterward. It provides assurance that the sender's identity and involvement in the communication cannot be denied, bolstering accountability and trust in digital transactions. This security service relies on cryptographic techniques to create irrefutable evidence of message origin and transmission, thus deterring dishonest behavior and facilitating dispute resolution. Implementing non-repudiation measures helps maintain integrity and credibility in electronic communications and transactions.

## 113. Answer: B

**Explanation:** Privacy by design emphasizes integrating privacy measures into systems and processes from the initial stages of development.

## 114. Answer: A

**Explanation:** Threat Modeling is a proactive approach used during the design phase of security architecture to pinpoint and rank potential security risks.

## 115. Answer: B

**Explanation:** SSL/TLS protocols encrypt web traffic to secure data exchanged between web browsers and servers. This encryption ensures confidentiality and integrity, protecting sensitive information from unauthorized access or tampering. SSL/TLS certificates validate the identity of servers, assuring users of secure connections and mitigating risks of interception or data breaches. SSL/TLS enhances trust and privacy for online transactions and browsing activities by establishing secure communication channels.

## 116. Answer: B

**Explanation:** SSO allows users to use the same set of credentials to access multiple systems, reducing the need for multiple logins.

**117. Answer: C**

**Explanation:** A security baseline sets a minimum level of security for systems and applications, ensuring a standardized and secure configuration.

**118. Answer: C**

**Explanation:** The Endorsement Key, is a unique pair of cryptographic keys pre-installed during manufacturing. Once set, the EK remains unchanged and cannot be altered or modified. It serves as a foundational element in secure boot processes and cryptographic operations, ensuring the integrity and authenticity of hardware components. This static nature enhances security by providing a trusted root for various cryptographic operations and verifications.

**119. Answer: C**

**Explanation:** Secure Coding Guidelines are principles and practices implemented during software development to detect and mitigate potential security flaws in the code.

**120. Answer: B**

**Explanation:** Quantitative Risk Analysis assigns numerical values to risks, enabling a more objective evaluation of their potential impact and likelihood.

**121. Answer: C**

**Explanation:** Data Loss Prevention (DLP) technology is designed to oversee and manage the flow of sensitive data within an organization, aiming to block unauthorized disclosure or leakage.

**122. Answer: C**

**Explanation:** The TPM is involved in security functions such as binding hard drives and sealing system configurations but does not directly protect against electromagnetic interference.

**123. Answer: B**

**Explanation:** User education and awareness training can help users identify and avoid phishing emails and malicious attachments, thus preventing malware infection.

**124. Answer: B**

**Explanation:** The Digital Signature Standard (DSS), introduced by NIST, outlines protocols and criteria for implementing secure digital signatures. It offers guidelines for the generation and verification of digital signatures, ensuring their integrity and authenticity. Compliance with DSS helps establish a secure framework for digital transactions and communications, fostering trust in electronic signatures' validity and reliability. DSS standards enhance security and legal validity in digital document exchanges and online transactions.

**125. Answer: A**

**Explanation:** Data encryption protects sensitive information at rest (stored in the cloud). And in transit (during transfer). This ensures unauthorized access even if data is intercepted.

**126. Answer: B**

**Explanation:** A digital signature ensures that the message has not been modified (integrity) and confirms the sender's identity (authentication), providing non-repudiation as well.

**127. Answer: B**

**Explanation:** Regularly testing the disaster recovery plan identifies potential weaknesses and ensures a smooth recovery process in case of a disaster. Backups should be stored off-site to safeguard data from physical incidents.

**128. Answer: C**

**Explanation:** Password managers help users create, store, and manage strong, unique passwords for different accounts, reducing the risk of password breaches.

**129. Answer: B**

**Explanation:** PKI provides several security services, including confidentiality, access control, integrity, authentication, and non-repudiation. Virus scanning is not a service provided by PKI; it is typically handled by antivirus software or other security solutions.

**130. Answer: C**

**Explanation:** ISO 27001 is a standard that sets out requirements for establishing, implementing, maintaining, and continually improving an Information Security Management System (ISMS). This framework helps organizations systematically manage sensitive information, assess risks, and implement appropriate security controls. By adhering to ISO 27001, businesses can establish robust governance structures for protecting their information assets and ensuring compliance with relevant regulations and best practices.

**131. Answer: C**

**Explanation:** Data at rest refers to data that is stored on non-volatile storage devices, such as hard drives or databases.

**132. Answer: A**

**Explanation:** RSA, named after its inventors Rivest, Shamir, and Adleman, is a widely adopted cryptographic algorithm used for securing email communication through public-key cryptography.

**133. Answer: B**

**Explanation:** An email client is part of an email infrastructure, not a PKI. A PKI includes entities and functions such as certification authorities, registration authorities, certificate repositories, certificate revocation systems, key backup and recovery systems, automatic key updates, management of key histories, timestamping, and client-side software.

**134. Answer: B**

**Explanation:** Role-Based Access Control (RBAC) assigns permissions to users based on their job roles, simplifying access management and minimizing administrative overhead.

**135. Answer: B**

**Explanation:** Cross-certification is undertaken by CAs to establish a trust relationship where they rely upon each other's digital certificates and public keys as if they had issued them, allowing for secure communication between different entities that each have their own PKI.

**136. Answer: C**

**Explanation:** The X.509 standard outlines how digital certificates are created, including the specific fields and the valid values that can populate those fields, such as serial number, version number, and identity information.

**137. Answer: B**

**Explanation:** The primary objective of code review in the software development process is to identify and fix security vulnerabilities in the code, along with other potential issues such as bugs, logical errors, and deviations from coding standards. Code reviews help ensure that the code is of high quality, maintainable, and secure before it is deployed. While enhancing the user interface and accelerating the development process can be secondary benefits, the main goal is to catch and address problems early in the development cycle to prevent issues in production. Ignoring security concerns until after deployment is not a best practice and can lead to significant security risks.

**138. Answer: B**

**Explanation:** The Online Certificate Status Protocol (OCSP) is being utilized more frequently than CRLs because it provides real-time validation of certificates, automatically checking the CRL maintained by the CA in the background.

**139. Answer: B**

**Explanation:** A CRL is maintained by the CA and is a list of every certificate that has been revoked, whether due to key compromise or incorrect issuance, and is periodically updated to inform users of invalid certificates.

**140. Answer: C**

**Explanation:** The RA performs certification registration duties by establishing and confirming the identity of an individual, initiating the certification process with a CA on behalf of an end user, and performing certificate life-cycle management functions.

**141. Answer: B**

**Explanation:** Reporting suspicious websites to the security team allows them to investigate and potentially block them to prevent phishing attacks.

## 142. Answer: B

**Explanation:** Risk management is a proactive approach that involves identifying potential threats, analyzing their likelihood and impact, and implementing appropriate controls to reduce or eliminate those risks.

## 143. Answer: C

**Explanation:** Data encryption at rest involves encoding data stored in cloud storage, rendering it unreadable to unauthorized individuals, even if they access the storage system.

## 144. Answer: C

**Explanation:** The Certificate Authority (CA) is the trusted third-party or server responsible for creating and signing digital certificates, which binds an individual's identity to their public key and takes liability for the authenticity of that individual.

## 145. Answer: B

**Explanation:** A comprehensive Incident Response (IR) plan establishes a structured approach for recognizing, isolating, eliminating, and recovering from security breaches. This plan aims to mitigate harm and swiftly restore regular operations through predefined procedures and protocols. Organizations can effectively manage incidents, minimize disruptions, and safeguard sensitive data by documenting these steps. The IR plan serves as a blueprint for coordinated actions, ensuring a timely and efficient response to security threats.

## 146. Answer: B

**Explanation:** PKI is designed to establish a level of trust within an environment, allowing dispersed people to communicate securely and predictably by using public key cryptography and the X.509 standard for authentication across different networks and the internet.

## 147. Answer: D

**Explanation:** MAC authentication, which involves using a symmetric key, provides the weakest form of authentication because it is not bound to a user but rather to a system or device. This differs from methods like HMAC, CBC-MAC, and CMAC, which provide stronger authentication by ensuring that only someone with the key can verify the message's integrity and authenticity.

**148. Answer: C**

**Explanation:** In CMAC, a symmetric key generates subkeys utilized to encrypt message blocks individually. Similar to CBC-MAC but with added security measures, CMAC ensures data origin authentication and integrity verification.

**149. Answer: C**

**Explanation:** Larger message digest values in hashing algorithms provide greater resistance to brute-force attacks, including birthday attacks. The larger the output (bit size) of the hash function, the lower the probability of an attacker finding two different messages that produce the same hash value.

**150. Answer: A**

**Explanation:** Security models provide frameworks for developing and deploying secure systems and structures. They offer guidelines and principles to ensure robust security measures are in place, addressing potential threats and vulnerabilities. By following these models, organizations can build defenses against cyberattacks and safeguard sensitive data effectively. Security models serve as blueprints for designing resilient architectures that prioritize confidentiality, integrity, and availability.

**151. Answer: C**

**Explanation:** PGP is commonly used for securing email communication through the use of public-key cryptography.

**152. Answer: A**

**Explanation:** In CBC-MAC, the message is encrypted with a symmetric block cipher in CBC mode, and the output of the final block of ciphertext is used as the MAC. This MAC is then appended to the plaintext message and sent to the receiver, who can verify the message's integrity using the same key.

## 153. Answer: B

**Explanation:** SHA-1 was found vulnerable to collisions, where two different messages produce the same hash value. New versions such as SHA-2 and SHA-3 were developed to mitigate this, offering improved security and resilience against collision attacks.

## 154. Answer: A

**Explanation:** A Message Authentication Code (MAC) is used for data origin authentication, integrity checking, and detecting unauthorized message alterations. However, it is not used for data encryption, which is the process of transforming information to make it unreadable to unauthorized users.

## 155. Answer: A

**Explanation:** HMAC uses a symmetric key in conjunction with the original message to produce a MAC value. The symmetric key is concatenated with the message, and the result is put through a hashing algorithm to generate the MAC, which is then appended to the message. The symmetric key usage guarantees that only individuals possessing the key can authenticate the message's integrity and authenticity.

## 156. Answer: C

**Explanation:** Parity bits are not effective against intentional unauthorized modifications because an intruder who captures and alters a message can recalculate a new parity value to include the changes. The receiver would then not be able to detect that the message had been tampered with.

## 157. Answer: C

**Explanation:** Zero-knowledge proof allows the prover to demonstrate possession of a certain knowledge (like a private key) without revealing the secret itself.

## 158. Answer: B

**Explanation:** Misuse case testing is aimed at understanding how an adversary might attempt to misuse or subvert software. It allows developers to identify potential security threats and implement controls to mitigate them, enhancing the software's security.

### 159. Answer: B

**Explanation:** Software controls are intended to prevent unauthorized access and protect against security threats, not facilitate them. They are implemented to secure various aspects of software operation, such as managing input, encryption, and interprocess communication.

### 160. Answer: C

**Explanation:** In software development, both functionality and security are crucial and should be given equal importance. Functionality ensures that the software performs the intended tasks and meets user requirements, while security ensures that the software is protected against threats and vulnerabilities. Neglecting either aspect can lead to software that is either unusable or insecure, which can result in significant risks and failures. Therefore, a balanced approach that addresses both functionality and security is essential for creating robust and reliable software.

### 161. Answer: D

**Explanation:** This phrase metaphorically describes an environment with strong perimeter defenses, such as firewalls and intrusion detection systems, but once an attacker breaches the perimeter, the internal security is weak, making it easy to exploit vulnerabilities.

### 162. Answer: C

**Explanation:** In the past, implementing security during the software development stages was not viewed as essential, which is why many developers today do not practice these procedures. The lack of historic emphasis on security during development has contributed to this trend.

### 163. Answer: B

**Explanation:** The rush to release products fast, usually because customers want them quickly, can lead to skipping important steps to make sure they're secure. This rush means there might not be enough time to properly plan, design, and test the security of the software. As a result, the software might have weaknesses or flaws that hackers could exploit to harm.

## 164. Answer: C

**Explanation:** When installing security applications or devices, they should default to "No Access". This means they should not permit any actions or access until they have been specifically configured to grant such permissions, enhancing the overall security posture.

## 165. Answer: C

**Explanation:** Vendors often ship products with default settings that prioritize user friendliness and functionality over security. They do this to make the installation and configuration process easier for the user, which can result in a less secure initial setup.

## 166. Answer: B

**Explanation:** Sometimes, administrators don't stay informed about new security problems and updates needed for their systems. This often leads to systems not getting important fixes, making them vulnerable to attacks. Hackers might take advantage of these weaknesses to cause problems if they aren't fixed.

## 167. Answer: B

**Explanation:** The best way to minimize the need for security patches is by developing software properly from the start, which involves secure coding practices and thorough testing to prevent vulnerabilities

## 168. Answer: C

**Explanation:** The primary purpose of the SDLC is to put in place repeatable and predictable processes that help ensure functionality, cost, quality, and delivery schedule requirements are met for software development projects.

## 169. Answer: D

**Explanation:** Attack surface analysis is a security task performed during the Design phase, not a main phase of the SDLC. The main phases are requirements gathering, design, development, testing, operations, and maintenance.

**170. Answer: C**

**Explanation:** A security risk assessment should first be carried out during the requirements gathering phase to define security requirements and assess potential threats and their associated consequences.

**171. Answer: C**

**Explanation:** The primary output from the design phase is a design that outlines how the product will fulfill the identified requirements from the requirements gathering phase.

**172. Answer: B**

**Explanation:** Fuzzing is a testing technique that involves sending large amounts of malformed, unexpected, or random data to a software application to uncover vulnerabilities.

**173. Answer: B**

**Explanation:** Static analysis is a technique aimed at identifying software defects or security policy violations by examining the code without executing the program.

**174. Answer: B**

**Explanation:** The operations and maintenance phase involves deploying the software to a production environment and addressing any newly discovered problems or vulnerabilities.

**175. Answer: B**

**Explanation:** Verification in the SDLC determines if the product accurately represents and meets the specifications, ensuring that the product was built correctly.

**176. Answer: B**

**Explanation:** A Privacy Impact Rating helps assess how sensitive the data handled by software is during its development lifecycle.

**177. Answer: B**

**Explanation:** A zero-day vulnerability is one without a pre-existing fix, discovered at any stage during or after the Software Development Life Cycle

(SDLC).

**178. Answer: D**

**Explanation:** The waterfall methodology uses a linear-sequential life-cycle approach, meaning that each phase must be completed in its entirety before the next phase can begin. This methodology is known for being very rigid and can be ineffective for complex projects due to the difficulty of integrating changes once the project is underway.

**179. Answer: C**

**Explanation:** The V-shaped methodology emphasizes the verification and validation of the product at each phase. It provides a formal method of developing testing plans as each coding phase is executed, which increases the chance of success compared to the waterfall methodology.

**180. Answer: D**

**Explanation:** Static is not a type of prototyping model. Prototyping models typically include Rapid, Evolutionary, and Operational models, which involve iterative development and refinement of prototypes to meet project requirements. However, "Static" does not represent a commonly recognized prototyping model.

**181. Answer: B**

**Explanation:** The Incremental methodology involves multiple development cycles for a piece of software. In each iteration, a working version of the software is created and progresses through subsequent phases, with each release delivering an operational product.

**182. Answer: D**

**Explanation:** The spiral methodology is renowned for its emphasis on risk analysis throughout the software development process. It involves iterative development and prototyping, but its primary focus is on identifying and mitigating risks associated with the project, making option D the most accurate choice.

**183. Answer: B**

**Explanation:** The Rapid Application Development (RAD), this methodology relies more on the use of rapid prototyping than on extensive upfront planning. This allows for quick development of software and the ability to adapt to changing requirements in a shorter timeframe.

**184. Answer: C**

**Explanation:** Scrum is an agile methodology that uses fixed-duration development intervals called sprints. These sprints typically last two weeks and promise the delivery of a specific set of features. Scrum allows for product features to be added, changed, or removed at clearly defined points.

**185. Answer: B**

**Explanation:** Pair programming in Extreme Programming (XP) involves two programmers working together collaboratively on the same code. Both programmers actively participate in writing and reviewing the code simultaneously, sharing ideas and providing immediate feedback to each other. This practice is not about one person dictating while the other types; rather, it emphasizes teamwork, communication, and joint problem-solving to enhance code quality and productivity.

**186. Answer: B**

**Explanation:** Kanban is a development methodology that stresses visual tracking of all tasks so that the team knows what to prioritize and when in order to deliver the right features at the right time. It often uses boards with tasks represented as sticky notes moving through various production phases.

**187. Answer: C**

**Explanation:** DevOps is the practice of incorporating development, IT, and Quality Assurance (QA) Staff into software development projects. The goal is to align their incentives and enable frequent, efficient, and reliable releases of software products while improving collaboration and reducing friction between teams.

**188. Answer: A**

**Explanation:** Capability Maturity Model Integration (CMMI) provides a comprehensive, integrated set of guidelines for developing products and software. It addresses the different phases of a software development life cycle. It aims to help software vendors improve their development processes by providing an evolutionary path from an ad hoc approach to a more disciplined and repeatable method.

### 189. Answer: B

**Explanation:** Customers can use CMMI to evaluate a software vendor's security engineering practices and identify ways to improve them, which can assist in the decision-making process when selecting a software vendor.

### 190. Answer: C

**Explanation:** Following the CMMI model, a company is expected to improve software quality, reduce the life cycle of development, and provide better project management capabilities, among other benefits.

### 191. Answer: B

**Explanation:** At the repeatable level, a company establishes a formal management structure and implements change control and quality assurance processes, allowing for the repetition of successful processes across projects.

### 192. Answer: B

**Explanation:** The DevOps maturity model is focused on how effectively an organization integrates its development and operations teams, emphasizing culture and people in addition to development and business issues.

### 193. Answer: C

**Explanation:** The Software product management maturity model focuses on the business issues surrounding the development of software products, including market conditions, product lines and portfolios, and partnering agreements.

### 194. Answer: B

**Explanation:** Change management is a systematic approach that aims to regulate changes deliberately within projects, including software development projects, to ensure that they are carefully analyzed, approved, and properly incorporated without adversely affecting the original functionality.

**195. Answer: C**

**Explanation:** Changes to the production code must first be applied to the test version, undergoing documentation and testing processes to ensure they do not adversely impact the product's functionality.

**196. Answer: C**

**Explanation:** The librarian is responsible for providing the production code. Programmers should not change production code directly; instead, they should submit the new, tested code to the librarian, who then manages the production code updates.

**197. Answer: D**

**Explanation:** The contract serves to confirm that the customer agrees to the design, requirements, and specifications and acknowledges that any additional changes requested will incur extra costs to the customer.

**198. Answer: C**

**Explanation:** Without proper change control, customers can continually request changes without bearing the associated costs, leading to scope creep, where the project expands beyond its original boundaries, causing delays and potential financial losses for the vendor.

**199. Answer: C**

**Explanation:** The team leader should notify the project manager about the additional time needed to implement the change in the project and outline the necessary steps to mitigate its impact on other components.

**200. Answer: C**

**Explanation:** Uncontrolled changes can lead to incompatibilities between different components of the product, which can result in accountability issues and potential job risks for those involved, especially if the changes were not approved by management.

**201. Answer: C**

**Explanation:** A process for managing changes should be established at the outset of a project to ensure clarity on how changes are handled and the expectations when a change request is initiated.

**202. Answer: B**

**Explanation:** The necessary steps for a change control process include making a formal request for a change, analyzing the request, recording it, submitting it for approval, developing the change, and reporting results to management.

**203. Answer: C**

**Explanation:** If the changes to a system are significant, the functionality and level of protection may need to be reevaluated (certified) and management would need to approve the overall system, including the new changes (accreditation).

**204. Answer: C**

**Explanation:** SSH (Secure Shell) is a protocol used for securely managing network devices by providing encrypted communication and authentication.

**205. Answer: C**

**Explanation:** Emphasizes the importance of enforcing good change management practices to secure development endpoints. Cautions against giving software engineers unfettered privileged access as they may make unauthorized changes to their workstations.

**206. Answer: B**

**Explanation:** A VPN is the best solution for remote access to an isolated development network.

**207. Answer: C**

**Explanation:** Insufficient separation between development and production environments can result in security vulnerabilities, potentially allowing attackers to compromise source code.

**208. Answer: B**

**Explanation:** Software Configuration Management enables systematic oversight of modifications during software development to uphold the software's integrity and trackability across its lifecycle.

**209. Answer: C**

**Explanation:** SCM systems handle tasks like managing concurrent changes, version control, and synchronization of software components but do not typically involve automatic code generation.

### 210. Answer: B

**Explanation:** An "air-gapped" network is completely isolated from external networks, minimizing the risk of unauthorized access to sensitive data stored in code repositories.

### 211. Answer: B

**Explanation:** SSH can be configured for use with code repositories to ensure that all traffic is encrypted, even inside the intranet, which helps to mitigate the risk of data being intercepted or sniffed.

### 212. Answer: B

**Explanation:** Software escrow is a framework where a third party keeps a copy of the source code and other materials, releasing them to the customer only under specific circumstances, such as if the vendor goes out of business, ensuring the customer's ability to maintain and update the software.

### 213. Answer: A

**Explanation:** The source code may be considered the vendor's intellectual property, and handing it over to the customer could mean giving away trade secrets. The vendor employs skilled individuals to develop the code and typically provides compiled code to protect its intellectual property.

### 214. Answer: D

**Explanation:** Remote code execution is not listed in the OWASP Top 10 list from 2017. The list includes issues like Injection, Broken Authentication, and Sensitive Data Exposure, but Remote Code Execution is not specifically mentioned.

### 215. Answer: C

**Explanation:** The main goal of secure coding is to develop software that is free from defects, particularly those that could be exploited by adversaries to cause harm or loss.

### 216. Answer: C

**Explanation:** The Software Engineering Institute (SEI) at Carnegie Mellon University consistently produces good coding standards, including a top 10 list of secure coding practices.

## 217. Answer: A

**Explanation:** By default, all requests should be denied unless there is a specific and valid reason to allow them. This helps to minimize the attack surface and reduce the risk of unauthorized access or exploitation of vulnerabilities in the system.

## 218. Answer: C

**Explanation:** Elliptic Curve Cryptosystems (ECC) are more efficient than RSA and are suitable for devices with limited processing capacity, storage, power supply, and bandwidth.

## 219. Answer: B

**Explanation:** Public Key Infrastructure relies on asymmetric key algorithms for secure communication, where each user has a pair of keys: a public key for encryption and a private key for decryption. This infrastructure facilitates authentication, encryption, and digital signatures, ensuring the confidentiality, integrity, and authenticity of data transmissions.

## 220. Answer: A

**Explanation:** A one-way function is a mathematical function that is easy to compute in one direction but computationally difficult to invert. In the context of asymmetric algorithms, such as RSA or Diffie-Hellman, one-way functions are used for encryption.

## 221. Answer: C

**Explanation:** Prioritizing high-performance code over secure code is not a part of the SEI's top 10 secure coding practices. The focus is on security and quality rather than performance alone.

## 222. Answer: C

**Explanation:** Machine language is the most primitive form of programming language. It is represented in a binary format and was used as the sole method of programming in the early 1950s. It is the format that a computer's processor can directly understand and work with.

**223. Answer: C**

**Explanation:** Assembly language uses symbols called mnemonics to represent the complicated binary codes of machine-level instructions. This allows programmers to use commands like ADD, PUSH, POP, etc., instead of binary codes.

**224. Answer: C**

**Explanation:** High-level languages abstract away the low-level intricacies of system architecture, allowing programmers to focus on their objectives with syntax that is more akin to human languages.

**225. Answer: B**

**Explanation:** Fourth-generation languages are designed to enhance the natural language approach, requiring significantly less manual coding to perform specific tasks compared to third-generation languages.

**226. Answer: A**

**Explanation:** The ultimate target of fifth-generation languages is to create software that can solve problems by itself, thereby eliminating the need for traditional programming expertise.

**227. Answer: A**

**Explanation:** Compilers are tools that transform high-level language statements into the necessary machine-level format, such as.exe or.dll files, for specific processors to understand and execute.

**228. Answer: B**

**Explanation:** While interpreted programming languages improve portability, a major disadvantage is that they require an interpreter to be installed on the local machine to run the program.

**229. Answer: C**

**Explanation:** Garbage collection is an automated memory management task that identifies and deallocates memory blocks that are no longer in use, helping to maintain system stability and efficiency.

**230. Answer: C**

**Explanation:** In OOP, an object is an instance of a class, inheriting the class's attributes and capable of performing methods or functions defined by the class.

**231. Answer: C**

**Explanation:** Low coupling indicates that a module does not heavily depend on other modules to perform its tasks, which makes it easier to understand, maintain, and reuse.

**232. Answer: B**

**Explanation:** DCE was developed by the Open Software Foundation, now known as the Open Group, and was one of the first attempts to standardize communication in a heterogeneous client/server environment. It provided a set of management services and a communications layer based on Remote Procedure Call (RPC).

**233. Answer: C**

**Explanation:** The directory service in DCE allows users, servers, and resources to be located anywhere on the network by providing the network address and other necessary information when given the name of the resource.

**234. Answer: B**

**Explanation:** In the CORBA model, ORBs are responsible for managing all communications between components, which allows them to interact in a distributed, heterogeneous environment. ORBs work independently of the platforms where the objects reside, offering greater interoperability.

**235. Answer: B**

**Explanation:** DCOM stands for Distributed Component Object Model. It extends the Component Object Model (COM) to support distributed Inter-Process Communication (IPC).

**236. Answer: B**

**Explanation:** SOAP, or Simple Object Access Protocol, is an advantage in distributed computing because it uses XML and HTTP, which are already standard web formats. This helps ensure compatibility and facilitates communication through firewalls since HTTP is commonly allowed.

**237. Answer: C**

**Explanation:** Java Platform, Enterprise Edition (Java EE) is the technology that provides a framework for developing enterprise software mainly in the Java programming language. It is designed for large-scale, multitier network applications.

**238. Answer: B**

**Explanation:** SOA provides standardized access to commonly needed application functionality and procedures across various environments, allowing different applications to call upon and use centralized services.

**239. Answer: D**

**Explanation:** DCOM is not a component of web services in an SOA. Simple Object Access Protocol (SOAP), Web Services Description Language (WSDL), and Universal Description, Discovery, and Integration (UDDI) are all components used in web services for SOA.

**240. Answer: B**

**Explanation:** Universal Description, Discovery, and Integration (UDDI) is an XML-based registry that allows service providers to register their services and service consumers to locate those services within an SOA environment.

**241. Answer: B**

**Explanation:** Applications written for the.NET framework are compiled to an intermediate code type, Common Language Runtime (CLR), and then executed at runtime within an application virtual machine. This provides memory management, exception handling, and security services, among other functionalities.

**242. Answer: A**

**Explanation:** Mobile code is primarily used for legitimate reasons, such as executing web browser applets in the background to download additional content for the web page, such as plug-ins that allow users to view a video.

**243. Answer: B**

**Explanation:** Java is platform-independent because it creates bytecode, which is not processor-specific. The Java Virtual Machine (JVM) then converts the bytecode to machine-level code that the processor on that particular system can understand.

## 244. Answer: B

**Explanation:** An applet in Java is a small component, commonly run in a user's web browser, which can be part of a web page and executes as soon as it arrives.

## 245. Answer: B

**Explanation:** The sandbox in Java's security model provides a virtual machine, which is an enclosed environment that strictly limits the applet's access to any system resources to ensure the applet code stays within its confined area.

## 246. Answer: C

**Explanation:** Java applets can be a security risk if developers fail to manage security properly, potentially allowing them to access sensitive system resources or escape the sandbox.

## 247. Answer: B

**Explanation:** ActiveX is a Microsoft technology used to create self-sufficient programs, similar to Java applets that can be executed in the Windows environment and can add extra functionality to web pages.

## 248. Answer: C

**Explanation:** The main security issue with ActiveX controls is that they share the privilege levels of the current user on a system. A malicious ActiveX control could compromise a system's security by exploiting vulnerabilities or weaknesses in the control's code. Once executed, it may gain elevated privileges or access to system resources beyond what is intended, allowing it to perform unauthorized actions or execute malicious code. This could lead to unauthorized access, data theft, system manipulation, or the installation of additional malware, ultimately compromising the overall security of the system.

## 249. Answer: C

**Explanation:** The main security difference is that Java applets execute within a sandbox, limiting their access to system resources, whereas ActiveX controls rely on Authenticode technology, which uses digital certificates for security.

**250. Answer: C**

**Explanation:** Microsoft has discontinued support for ActiveX in its Edge web browser because of the inherent security flaws in ActiveX technology. These vulnerabilities can compromise system security and facilitate the propagation of worms.

**251. Answer: B**

**Explanation:** Port 80 is used for HTTP traffic, and port 443 is used for HTTPS traffic, which is secure HTTP. These are the standard ports used for web traffic, and companies usually need to open them on their firewalls to allow access to their web servers.

**252. Answer: D**

**Explanation:** Off-the-shelf software can be a good choice because many commercial and free options are available, and they are often developed and tested with appropriate security in mind. However, it does not guarantee more security or eliminate all vulnerabilities, and it offers less customization than an in-house developed application.

**253. Answer: C**

**Explanation:** Web-based administrative interfaces can be convenient, but they also provide an entry point into the system for unauthorized users, making them a significant security risk.

**254. Answer: B**

**Explanation:** Attackers commonly mine usernames via search engines or by using common usernames and trying to log into targeted sites. This method is used to gain unauthorized access to systems that hold sensitive information.

**255. Answer: C**

**Explanation:** This type of attack is known as a path or directory traversal or "dot-dot-slash" attack. It involves exploiting a vulnerability that allows an attacker to access file directories on the server that should not be accessible through the web interface.

## 256. Answer: B

**Explanation:** The best practice is to exchange all authentication information, and all authenticated content via a secure mechanism, which typically means encrypting the credential and the channel of communication through Transport Layer Security (TLS).

## 257. Answer: B

**Explanation:** Unicode encoding is a technique used by attackers to bypass filtering techniques and make requests that might otherwise be blocked by using different representations of characters that are processed by the system as valid commands.

## 258. Answer: D

**Explanation:** Non-persistent XSS vulnerabilities occur when an attacker tricks a victim into processing a URL programmed with a rogue script to steal sensitive information, unlike persistent XSS vulnerabilities. The attacker's malicious script is stored on the server and executed whenever a user accesses the stored content.

## 259. Answer: B

**Explanation:** Cookies are used to keep track of the state of a user's connection with the server, as HTTP does not maintain the state between different requests. Cookies can be either session cookies (stored in memory) or persistent cookies (stored as files).

## 260. Answer: D

**Explanation:** Failing securely means that when an error occurs, the system should behave in a predictable manner that does not compromise security. This typically involves displaying generic error messages that do not reveal internal system details or vulnerabilities.

## 261. Answer: B

**Explanation:** A DBMS is a suite of programs used to manage large sets of structured data and control the security parameters, ensuring data integrity, access control, and confidentiality.

**262. Answer: C**

**Explanation:** The relational database model is the most widely used today and organizes information using attributes (columns) and tuples (rows) in table formats.

**263. Answer: B**

**Explanation:** A primary key is used within a database table to link all the data within a record to a unique value for easy and accurate retrieval.

**264. Answer: C**

**Explanation:** Databases are designed to allow the sharing of data with multiple users, and one of their characteristics is to support multi-user access.

**265. Answer: C**

**Explanation:** An ODBMS is dynamic and bundles data with procedures, enabling objects to be created with data and methods for processing that data.

**266. Answer: B**

**Explanation:** Polyinstantiation enables the creation of multiple data instances with identical primary keys but differentiated by varying security levels. This technique is commonly used in database security to manage access control and enforce data confidentiality requirements for different users or security contexts. It ensures that users with different clearance levels can access data tailored to their specific security needs, minimizing the risk of unauthorized disclosure or exposure of sensitive information.

**267. Answer: B**

**Explanation:** A data dictionary is a centralized tool that contains metadata about the data within the database, including data element definitions and schema objects.

**268. Answer: C**

**Explanation:** Roles are used in database security to define specific permissions and streamline access control, ensuring that users and processes can only access the database indirectly through role accounts.

### 269. Answer: B

**Explanation:** The ACID test comprises Atomicity (all-or-nothing principle), Consistency (adherence to integrity constraints), Isolation (independent transaction execution), and Durability (persistence of transaction effects).

### 270. Answer: D

**Explanation:** Malware commonly spreads by email, sharing media, and downloading from the internet. Manual attacks are less common today due to automation. Encrypted messaging apps are not mentioned as a common method for malware distribution.

### 271. Answer: B

**Explanation:** A rootkit is a set of tools installed on a compromised system to provide an attacker with administrator or root-level access. It often includes a backdoor for easy access and other tools for capturing credentials and covering tracks.

### 272. Answer: C

**Explanation:** A virus is a type of malware that requires a host application to replicate. It cannot self-replicate without attaching itself to another program or file.

### 273. Answer: B

**Explanation:** A polymorphic virus is designed to produce varied copies of itself to evade detection by antimalware programs, which may only have signatures for certain variants.

### 274. Answer: B

**Explanation:** Botnets, which are networks of compromised computers, are often used to perform DDoS attacks, distribute spam, or control systems as part of command-and-control infrastructure.

### 275. Answer: B

**Explanation:** While both viruses and worms are types of malware, the key distinction lies in their propagation methods. Viruses need a host file to attach to and rely on user interaction to spread, while worms are self-contained programs that can spread autonomously without needing to infect other files or rely on user actions.

**276. Answer: B**

**Explanation:** Heuristic detection analyzes the structure and behavior of code to assess the likelihood of it being malicious, allowing it to detect new malware not known by signatures.

**277. Answer: A**

**Explanation:** Rootkits are used to maintain control over a compromised system and cover the attacker's tracks, not to encrypt user files, which is typically a function of ransomware.

**278. Answer: B**

**Explanation:** Spyware covertly gathers sensitive information about a user without their knowledge, which can be used for malicious activities such as identity theft.

**279. Answer: B**

**Explanation:** Bayesian filtering applies statistical methods to the words in an email message to determine the likelihood of it being spam, which helps to filter out unwanted junk emails.

**280. Answer: C**

**Explanation:** According to the antimalware policy standards outlined, every workstation, server, and mobile device should have antimalware software installed to protect against malicious software.

**281. Answer: C**

**Explanation:** Antimalware policies and procedures should be reviewed annually to ensure they are up-to-date and effective against current malware threats.

**282. Answer: B**

**Explanation:** Antimalware files that contain updates, which include new signatures for virus detection, are called DAT files. These are data files with the file extension.dat.

## 283. Answer: C

**Explanation:** Antimalware solutions can be implemented at network entry points like mail servers, proxy servers, or firewalls, which are sometimes referred to as virus walls, to scan incoming traffic for malware.

## 284. Answer: D

**Explanation:** Virus scans should be automated and scheduled, as relying on manual scans is not sufficient for ensuring consistent protection.

## 285. Answer: B

**Explanation:** Assessing the security of acquired software includes looking at the vendor's reputation and the regularity of their patch pushes, as these factors correlate to a lower risk from the vendor's software.

## 286. Answer: B

**Explanation:** When the source code of acquired software is inaccessible, conducting an internal assessment via penetration testing becomes crucial for evaluating its security.

## 287. Answer: D

**Explanation:** Smaller or newer vendors with undeveloped or poorly documented processes may pose higher risks, particularly if their products are widely used.

## 288. Answer: B

**Explanation:** To mitigate the risks of acquired software without code reviews or penetration tests, organizations isolate it in secure subnetworks with strict configurations and monitoring.

## 289. Answer: C

**Explanation:** If a user detects a virus, they should notify the designated person within the organization, as outlined in the security awareness program's antimalware guidelines and expected user protocols.

**290. Answer: B**

**Explanation:** The operations department is tasked with ensuring that the correct policies, procedures, standards, and guidelines are in place and followed to maintain the necessary level of security. They balance ease of use, compliance with regulatory requirements, and cost constraints while achieving this level of security.

**291. Answer: B**

**Explanation:** Due care and due diligence are analogous to the "prudent person" concept, where a prudent person is seen as responsible, careful, cautious, and practical. A company that practices due care and due diligence is viewed in the same light.

**292. Answer: C**

**Explanation:** Companies and senior executives have legal obligations to ensure that resources are protected, safety measures are in place, and that security mechanisms are tested to guarantee they provide the necessary level of protection.

**293. Answer: B**

**Explanation:** Failure to meet operational security duties could expose the company to legal and liability ramifications extending beyond security breaches.

**294. Answer: C**

**Explanation:** Organizations must consider threats such as the disclosure of confidential data, theft of assets, corruption of data, interruption of services, and destruction of the physical or logical environment.

**295. Answer: A**

**Explanation:** Sensitive systems and operations must be safeguarded from unauthorized disclosure to maintain confidentiality. This entails implementing robust security measures to restrict access to confidential information and prevent unauthorized entry.

**296. Answer: B**

**Explanation:** Operational security concerns itself with configuration, performance, fault tolerance, security, and accounting and verification management. Employee hiring processes are typically a function of human resources, not operational security.

### 297. Answer: B

**Explanation:** Critical systems and operations are vital components that must consistently remain accessible to ensure the company's smooth operation.

### 298. Answer: B

**Explanation:** Operational security includes ensuring that physical and environmental concerns such as temperature and humidity controls are adequately addressed to protect sensitive equipment and data.

### 299. Answer: C

**Explanation:** Operational security involves the management of configuration, performance, fault tolerance, security, and accounting and verification to ensure compliance with proper standards of operations and regulatory requirements.

### 300. Answer: C

**Explanation:** The primary downside of El Gamal encryption lies in its performance, as it tends to be slower compared to other asymmetric encryption algorithms.

### 301. Answer: B

**Explanation:** Job rotation enables more than one person to understand the tasks and responsibilities of a specific job, providing backup and redundancy. It also serves as a detective control by helping to identify fraudulent activities, as someone else doing the job may notice irregularities.

### 302. Answer: C

**Explanation:** The original Diffie-Hellman algorithm is vulnerable to man-in-the-middle attacks because it does not authenticate the parties before they exchange public keys.

### 303. Answer: B

**Explanation:** RSA's versatility allows it to be used for digital signatures, key exchange, and encryption, making it a popular choice among asymmetric algorithms.

**304. Answer: C**

**Explanation:** Security administrators should not report to network administrators because the latter's focus on network availability and performance might be at odds with the former's focus on security, leading to potential conflicts of interest.

**305. Answer: C**

**Explanation:** The security administrator is tasked with implementing and maintaining security devices and software, as well as monitoring them to ensure they continue to be effective against new threats and vulnerabilities.

**306. Answer: B**

**Explanation:** Reviewing audit logs is essential as a detective control for identifying unauthorized access attempts and other security issues and ensuring that preventive controls like firewalls are functioning correctly.

**307. Answer: C**

**Explanation:** Authorization creep refers to the gradual increase of permissions attached to a user's account for legitimate reasons without subsequent review, leading to the accumulation of excessive privileges, which can pose security risks.

**308. Answer: B**

**Explanation:** When monitoring, administrators should assess whether users are accessing information and performing tasks outside of their necessary job duties. This may indicate the need for reevaluation and modification of their rights and permissions.

**309. Answer: B**

**Explanation:** Clipping levels are predefined thresholds that establish a baseline for normal violation activities by users. Exceeding this level triggers further investigation, signaling that the activity may be suspicious and warrants closer scrutiny.

**310. Answer: C**

**Explanation:** Implementing a layered approach to physical security aims to create multiple obstacles to discourage or impede intruders from accessing sensitive areas, such as the company's secret barbecue sauce recipe.

**311. Answer: D**

**Explanation:** It is important to have a diversity of controls so that if an intruder obtains one key or bypasses one control, they do not automatically gain access to all areas, thus preventing widespread access from a single compromise.

**312. Answer: B**

**Explanation:** Personnel within sensitive areas play a critical role in physical security controls as they can personally detect suspicious behavior and are trained on how to report such activity.

**313. Answer: B**

**Explanation:** Locks should not be the sole protection scheme because they can be picked or broken, and keys can be easily lost or duplicated, which could allow unauthorized access without detection.

**314. Answer: B**

**Explanation:** Cipher locks are keyless and use keypads or swipe cards to control access. They can provide a higher level of security and control by allowing combinations to be changed, specific codes to be locked out, and the initiation of a remote alarm under duress.

**315. Answer: B**

**Explanation:** The door delay functionality in cipher combination locks is designed to trigger an alarm if a door is held open for longer than a specified amount of time, alerting security personnel to possible suspicious activity.

**316. Answer: D**

**Explanation:** Automatic relocking after a set time is not listed as a common functionality of cipher combination locks. Key override, master keying, and hostage alarm are functionalities that improve performance and security.

**317. Answer: B**

**Explanation:** The combination of locks should be changed periodically to prevent intruders from guessing the code based on worn or frequently used keys, which may show signs of wear.

**318. Answer: C**

**Explanation:** The primary purpose of implementing bollards around a building is to deter vehicles from driving through exterior walls, providing a physical barrier that protects the building from such attacks.

**319. Answer: C**

**Explanation:** The audit trail for physical access control systems should include the date and time of access attempts, the entry point at which access was attempted, the user ID employed, and any unsuccessful access attempts, especially during unauthorized hours.

**320. Answer: D**

**Explanation:** Provisioning, as understood in the CISSP exam, involves all activities necessary to deliver new information services to users or user groups. This encompasses acquiring, configuring, and deploying these services.

**321. Answer: D**

**Explanation:** Asset inventory is critical because it helps organizations know exactly what they are defending. Without an accurate and timely inventory of hardware and software, it isn't easy to defend assets effectively.

**322. Answer: C**

**Explanation:** A primary security concern when tracking hardware is ensuring that new devices are free of back doors or piracy issues. This concern arises from reports of hardware being tampered with by manufacturers or third parties before reaching the organization.

**323. Answer: C**

**Explanation:** Application whitelisting is a widely accepted best practice for tracking software. It involves creating a list of authorized software that is allowed to execute on a device or set of devices, preventing the installation of unlicensed or unauthorized software.

## 324. Answer: B

**Explanation:** The asset management life cycle begins with the identification of a new requirement that existing assets are unable to satisfy. This triggers the process that eventually leads to the acquisition or development of a new asset.

## 325. Answer: B

**Explanation:** The purpose of a change management board is to ensure that new assets do not break any processes, introduce undue risks, or derail any ongoing projects. The board reviews and approves new assets, considering the broader impact on the organization.

## 326. Answer: D

**Explanation:** Hardware as a Service (HaaS) is not one of the three main cloud service models. The recognized models are Infrastructure as a Service (IaaS), Platform as a Service (PaaS), and Software as a Service (SaaS).

## 327. Answer: B

**Explanation:** A report should be generated with "no output" to confirm that the task was indeed carried out even when there was no new information to report. This helps prevent any confusion that might arise from a lack of communication.

## 328. Answer: B

**Explanation:** The primary goal of configuration management in terms of system security is to establish and maintain consistent baselines on all systems. This includes proper configurations that are responsive to the current threat and operational environments.

## 329. Answer: B

**Explanation:** A system reboot is typically triggered when the system detects a kernel failure and needs to shut down in a controlled manner to release resources and return to a more stable and safe state.

## 330. Answer: C

**Explanation:** A redundant Array of Independent Disks (RAID) is a technology used for redundancy and performance improvement. It combines several physical disks into logical arrays, enhancing read and write performance by using striping and providing redundancy through parity to restore data in case of a disk failure.

**331. Answer: B**

**Explanation:** Mean Time to Repair (MTTR) is the expected amount of time to fix a device and bring it back into production after its failure. MTBF refers to the average operational time between failures of a system, and RTO/RPO are objectives related to business continuity and disaster recovery planning.

**332. Answer: B**

**Explanation:** Fault-tolerant technologies are designed to ensure constant availability and operation of a system, even in the event of hardware failure. They are suited for mission-critical environments where downtime cannot be tolerated and can justify the higher cost associated with these technologies.

**333. Answer: C**

**Explanation:** A single point of failure is a critical component of a system or network that could cause a complete system failure or network outage if it fails. Protecting against single points of failure often involves implementing redundancy and fault tolerance.

**334. Answer: B**

**Explanation:** Hot swapping refers to the ability to replace or add components to a system without shutting it down, thus maintaining system availability and reducing downtime.

**335. Answer: C**

**Explanation:** RAID 5 is the most used RAID level that provides fault tolerance and improved performance. It uses striping with parity distributed across all the disks in the array, allowing the system to continue operating even if one disk fails.

**336. Answer: C**

**Explanation:** Service Level Agreements (SLAs) are formal documents that define the level of service expected from a service provider, including availability, performance, and other aspects of the service. They help in setting clear expectations and can guide the appropriate technology choices for meeting those expectations.

### 337. Answer: C

**Explanation:** Redundant paths between routers are implemented to prevent single points of failure. If one path or router fails, network traffic can be rerouted through alternative paths, thus maintaining network availability.

### 338. Answer: B

**Explanation:** Hierarchical Storage Management (HSM) is a data storage technique that automatically moves data between high-cost and low-cost storage media. The goal of HSM is to optimize the use of storage resources by storing less frequently accessed data on slower, more cost-effective media while keeping more frequently used data on faster, more expensive storage.

### 339. Answer: D

**Explanation:** Clustering technology involves grouping multiple servers to work together as a single system, improving availability and scalability. It offers load balancing by distributing the workload across multiple machines and provides redundancy, ensuring continued operation even if one server fails.

### 340. Answer: C

**Explanation:** An Intrusion Prevention System (IPS) detects, reports, and stops suspected intrusions, while an Intrusion Detection System (IDS) only detects and reports them. An IPS is designed to prevent the intrusion once it is detected, adding an extra level of protection.

### 341. Answer: B

**Explanation:** Key exchange involves the sender encrypting a symmetric key with the receiver's public key before transmission. Key agreement (as with Diffie-Hellman) uses public keys to derive a shared symmetric key.

### 342. Answer: C

**Explanation:** RSA (Rivest-Shamir-Adleman) is an asymmetric algorithm that is based on the difficulty of factoring large numbers. This factorization problem forms the basis of its security.

**343. Answer: C**

**Explanation:** NIST Special Publication 800-137 defines Information Security Continuous Monitoring (ISCM) as the practice of maintaining ongoing awareness of information security, vulnerabilities, and threats to support risk management decisions.

**344. Answer: C**

**Explanation:** Centralized patch management with testing of patches before their deployment is considered a best practice.

**345. Answer: C**

**Explanation:** Organizations may choose to outsource to an MSSP due to workforce shortages and resource constraints that make it challenging to maintain a full team of experienced security professionals in-house.

**346. Answer: C**

**Explanation:** It was created by Ron Rivest. RC5 is a block cipher that allows for a variety of parameters to be set for block size, key size, and the number of rounds used, giving developers extensive flexibility in its implementation. have block sizes of 32, 64, or 128 bits, key sizes of up to 2,048 bits, and up to 255 rounds.

**347. Answer: C**

**Explanation:** Vulnerability management is the cyclical process of identifying vulnerabilities, determining the risks they pose to the organization, and applying security controls that bring those risks to acceptable levels.

**348. Answer: C**

**Explanation:** A whitelist contains a set of known-good resources, such as IP addresses, domain names, or applications, and is used to ensure that only allowed resources can interact with or execute in the environment.

**349. Answer: C**

**Explanation:** Baselining is the process of establishing the normal patterns of behavior for a given network or system, which helps in reducing errors such as false positives and negatives by configuring the IDS to recognize what is normal for the organization.

### 350. Answer: C

**Explanation:** The first phase of the incident management process is 'Detect'. This phase involves realizing that there is a problem, which is crucial for a timely and effective incident response.

### 351. Answer: B

**Explanation:** The legal and security departments should manage the incident response policy. They work together to cover both the technical security issues and the legal issues surrounding criminal activities.

### 352. Answer: C

**Explanation:** The first step the incident response team should take is to investigate the report to determine if an actual crime has taken place.

### 353. Answer: B

**Explanation:** A virtual team comprises experts with other duties and assignments within the organization, which can lead to slower response times due to their primary responsibilities.

### 354. Answer: B

**Explanation:** An incident refers to a series of interconnected events that have adverse effects on the company, compromising its security stance.

### 355. Answer: B

**Explanation:** Incident handling aims to swiftly contain and reduce the impact of an incident while also preventing its escalation and recurrence.

### 356. Answer: B

**Explanation:** The last phase is 'Learn', where the incident response team reviews the incident and how it was handled to improve future response efforts.

### 357. Answer: D

**Explanation:** The Command and Control (C&C) stage occurs when malware communicates back to the attackers to confirm a successful attack and to request further instructions.

**358. Answer: D**

**Explanation:** Good security aims to protect the organization's assets and enhance productivity by providing a secure and predictable environment, allowing employees to focus on their tasks and discouraging attackers by making the target less appealing.

**359. Answer: C**

**Explanation:** All incidents should initially be treated as potential crime scenes because what might seem like a hardware failure, software defect, or accidental fire could have been caused by a malicious actor targeting the organization.

**360. Answer: A**

**Explanation:** The chain of custody is a history that shows how evidence was collected, analyzed, transported, and preserved to be presented in court. It is a critical component of the integrity and admissibility of evidence in legal proceedings.

**361. Answer: C**

**Explanation:** (ISC)² uses the term "digital forensics" as a synonym for computer forensics, network forensics, electronic data discovery, cyber forensics, and forensic computing. This term encompasses all domains where evidence is in a digital or electronic form.

**362. Answer: A**

**Explanation:** A forensic investigator must avoid rebooting the attacked system as it can corrupt viable evidence, change timestamps on key files, and erase footprints that the criminal may have left.

**363. Answer: B**

**Explanation:** Any agency that is responsible for seizing, accessing, storing, or transferring digital evidence is responsible for compliance with the

SWGDE principles, which aim to ensure consistency and integrity in the recovery of computer-based evidence.

**364. Answer: C**

**Explanation:** Motive, Opportunity, and Means (MOM) refer to the "whys" in crime and are used to understand the reason behind the crime (motive) and the circumstances allowing it (opportunity).

**365. Answer: B**

**Explanation:** The first phase in the common forensic investigation process is identification. This phase involves recognizing and determining the potential sources of digital evidence.

**366. Answer: D**

**Explanation:** The most volatile or fragile evidence should be collected first. This includes registers and cache, which are likely to lose their contents quickly upon system shutdown or alteration.

**367. Answer: C**

**Explanation:** Legal banners upon system login are crucial for establishing that a user does not expect privacy when using company equipment. The banner warns users that their activities may be monitored and can be used as evidence in court if necessary.

**368. Answer: C**

**Explanation:** The difference between enticement and entrapment is that entrapment involves tricking someone into committing a crime they had no intention of committing, which is neither legal nor ethical. Entrapment does not prove intent, while enticement is legal and involves attracting a suspect to commit a crime they were already predisposed to commit.

**369. Answer: D**

**Explanation:** The Recovery Time Objective (RTO) is the maximum allowable duration for restoring a business process after a disaster to prevent unacceptable consequences linked with a disruption in business continuity.

**370. Answer: C**

**Explanation:** RPO is the acceptable amount of data loss measured in time from a disaster, indicating the point where data must be recovered to avoid significant loss.

### 371. Answer: B

**Explanation:** Work Recovery Time (WRT) is the duration following the Recovery Time Objective (RTO), during which data and systems must be restored, tested, and brought back online for production use.

### 372. Answer: B

**Explanation:** A hot site is a leased or rented facility that is fully configured and operational within a short time frame, usually missing only the data and personnel.

### 373. Answer: C

**Explanation:** RC5 has a variable block size (32, 64, or 128 bits), key size (0 to 2040 bits), and number of rounds (0 to 255).

### 374. Answer: B

**Explanation:** MTD is the total amount of time a business process can be inoperative before an organization can no longer recover and resume normal operations.

### 375. Answer: C

**Explanation:** A cold site is the least expensive option for disaster recovery, but it requires the most time and effort to become functional after a disaster as it is an empty data center.

### 376. Answer: B

**Explanation:** Electronic vaulting involves making copies of files as they are modified and periodically transmitting them to an offsite backup site for storage and retrieval.

### 377. Answer: B

**Explanation:** A service bureau is a company that offers supplementary space, resources, and services, like call centers, to organizations during a disaster. This allows affected businesses to maintain critical operations and support their customers even when their facilities are unavailable due to the disaster. Service bureaus help ensure continuity of operations and minimize disruptions by providing essential infrastructure and support during times of crisis.

### 378. Answer: B

**Explanation:** A reciprocal agreement is an arrangement where two companies consent to allow each other to use their facilities if one of them is affected by a disaster.

### 379. Answer: B

**Explanation:** Due diligence is the act of gathering necessary information to make the best decision-making activities possible, specifically before a company purchases another company. Investigate all relevant aspects of the target company's past, present, and predictable future to avoid surprises.

### 380. Answer: B

**Explanation:** If a company does not perform due diligence to understand risks and fails to implement proper due care, it opens itself up to potential criminal charges, civil suits, regulatory fines, loss of market share, and more.

### 381. Answer: B

**Explanation:** Proximate cause is an act or omission that naturally and directly produces a consequence and is the superficial or obvious cause for an occurrence. It is an element used to determine negligence in court.

### 382. Answer: B

**Explanation:** Although the key size for DES is 64 bits, 8 bits are used for parity, which means the effective key length used for encryption and decryption is 56 bits.

### 383. Answer: C

**Explanation:** Security considerations should be taken into account for various contract types to ensure that regulatory, legal, and security requirements are properly integrated into the contractual clauses.

### 384. Answer: A

**Explanation:** Electronic Code Book (ECB) Mode is the simplest and fastest mode of DES operation and involves using the same key to encrypt each block. Encrypting large amounts of data can pose risks by preserving the patterns in the data, but it can reveal patterns when used to encrypt large amounts of data because the same key is used for each block of data.

**385. Answer: B**

**Explanation:** Vendor management encompasses establishing and overseeing relationships with vendors post-contract to ensure adherence to performance metrics, SLAs, and reporting structures. This ensures the continuity of secure and efficient operations.

**386. Answer: C**

**Explanation:** The Business Impact Analysis (BIA) identifies potential threats that the organization cannot entirely prevent. Insurance serves as a safeguard against such threats, mitigating risks and providing financial protection when preventive measures fall short.

**387. Answer: B**

**Explanation:** The probability of the threat and the potential loss. The decision on whether to obtain insurance and how much coverage to get should be based on the likelihood of the threat occurring and the potential financial impact, as identified during the Business Impact Analysis.

**388. Answer: C**

**Explanation:** The BCP team should collaborate with management to comprehend the existing insurance coverage, explore different insurance options, and understand the limits of each option, ensuring that any gaps in prevention are adequately covered by insurance.

**389. Answer: B**

**Explanation:** To insure losses caused by various cyber threats. Cyber insurance is a new type of coverage designed to protect against losses resulting from cyber incidents like denial-of-service attacks, malware damage, hackers, electronic theft, privacy-related lawsuits, and more.

**390. Answer: C**

**Explanation:** The security measures in place like IDS, antivirus software, firewalls, etc. Similar to how personal health factors affect individual insurance premiums, a company's security program and the measures it takes to protect against cyber threats play a role in determining its cyber insurance premiums.

### 391. Answer: B

**Explanation:** Business interruption insurance is tailored to cover specific expenses and lost earnings incurred when a company is temporarily unable to operate. It provides financial assistance for ongoing expenses and income loss during the downtime, helping the business to recover and resume operations smoothly.

### 392. Answer: C

**Explanation:** Accounts receivable insurance. This type of insurance covers part or all of the losses and costs if a company cannot collect on its accounts receivable for various reasons.

### 393. Answer: B

**Explanation:** Knowing what is expected of the company and what is expected from the insurance provider. It is crucial to read and understand the fine print of insurance policies to know the responsibilities of the company and the obligations of the insurance organization.

### 394. Answer: B

**Explanation:** Access controls are security features that primarily control how users and systems communicate and interact with other systems and resources. Their main function is to protect these systems and resources from unauthorized access and to ensure that the level of authorization is appropriate after successful authentication.

### 395. Answer: C

**Explanation:** In the context of access control, a subject is an active entity that requests access to an object or the data within an object. It could be a user, program, or process that accesses an object to accomplish a task

### 396. Answer: C

**Explanation:** An object is a passive entity that contains information or needed functionality. This could be a computer, database, file, computer program, directory, or field contained in a table within a database.

**397. Answer: D**

**Explanation:** When a user logs in and later attempts to access a file, if the file has a list of users and groups that have the right to access it and the user is not on this list, the user is denied access.

**398. Answer: A**

**Explanation:** In an access control system, users' permissions and rights are typically based on factors such as their identity, their clearance level, and their membership in certain groups. These factors determine what resources a user is allowed to access.

**399. Answer: D**

**Explanation:** While users, computer programs, and database fields are all entities that may require access to other network entities and resources, a router is a device that forwards data packets between computer networks, not an entity requesting access in the context of access control.

**400. Answer: B**

**Explanation:** After an authentication procedure has been completed, access controls play a role in determining the level of authorization that the subject has. This determines what specific resources the subject can access and with what permissions.

**401. Answer: C**

**Explanation:** Access controls give organizations the ability to control, restrict, monitor, and protect the availability of resources. This helps in preventing unauthorized access and ensuring that resources are available to authorized users when needed.

**402. Answer: B**

**Explanation:** Cipher Block Chaining (CBC), the mode adds a value based on the previous block to the encryption process, which hides any patterns by ensuring each block of ciphertext is dependent on all preceding blocks.

**403. Answer: C**

**Explanation:** When a file has a list of users and groups that have the right to access it, it represents a form of access control. This list is used to determine which users are authorized to view or interact with the file, thereby preventing unauthorized access.

**404. Answer: C**

**Explanation:** These are the core principles that every security control aims to uphold in order to protect a company's assets from various threats. Each security measure should provide at least one of these principles, and they are crucial for the productivity and safety of information systems.

**405. Answer: C**

**Explanation:** Blowfish is a block cipher that operates on 64-bit blocks of data and goes through 16 rounds of cryptographic functions. The key length can range from 32 bits up to 448 bits.

**406. Answer: B**

**Explanation:** DES is a symmetric block encryption algorithm that operates on 64-bit blocks of plaintext, converting them into 64-bit blocks of ciphertext. It uses a 64-bit key, with 56 bits being the true key and 8 bits for parity.

**407. Answer: B**

**Explanation:** The interception and alteration of an email from the secretary of state without detection or prevention constitutes a breach of integrity. This involves unauthorized data modification, directly compromising its accuracy and reliability.

**408. Answer: D**

**Explanation:** Rijndael, developed by Joan Daemen and Vincent Rijmen, was chosen out of five finalists as the Advanced Encryption Standard to replace DES. It supports key sizes of 128, 192, and 256 bits, and the number of rounds depends on the size of the block and the key length.

**409. Answer: C**

**Explanation:** Fault tolerance is a concept related to the availability principle, ensuring the continuity of access to resources. Encryption, database views, and logical and physical access controls are mechanisms that help maintain confidentiality by protecting sensitive information.

**410. Answer: B**

**Explanation:** It is important to identify which data is sensitive and, to what degree to implement appropriate security mechanisms. This helps in focusing resources on protecting critical information while not over-securing non-sensitive data.

**411. Answer: B**

**Explanation:** A strong stream cipher should have an unbiased keystream, meaning there should be an equal number of zeroes and ones. A keystream statistically biased in favor of zeroes or ones would indicate poor randomization and could potentially make the cipher easier to break.

**412. Answer: C**

**Explanation:** Initialization Vectors (IVs) in encryption prevent pattern formation by adding extra randomness. They ensure that identical plaintext does not produce the same ciphertext when encrypted with the same key.

**413. Answer: C**

**Explanation:** Configuring VPNs and using encryption protocols like IPSec to protect sensitive communications such as trade secrets and financial transactions, ensuring confidentiality.

**414. Answer: C**

**Explanation:** Authentication is the process by which a system verifies the identity of the subject, usually by requiring a piece of information that only the claimed identity should have, such as a password, cryptographic key, or biometric attribute.

**415. Answer: D**

**Explanation:** The three general factors used for authentication are something a person knows (like a password), something a person has (like a smart card), and something a person is (like a biometric feature).

**416. Answer: A**

**Explanation:** A Type I error, also known as a False Rejection Rate (FRR), occurs when a biometric system incorrectly rejects an authorized individual.

**417. Answer: C**

**Explanation:** The Authoritative System of Record (ASOR) is the location where identity information originates and is maintained. It should have the most up-to-date and reliable identity information.

**418. Answer: B**

**Explanation:** In the context of a network protocol stack, MAC stands for Media Access Control, which refers to data link layer functionality and address type within a network protocol stack. The other MAC acronyms stand for different concepts.

**419. Answer: C**

**Explanation:** The crossover error rate (CER) or equal error rate (EER) represents the point at which the false rejection rate (Type I error) equals the false acceptance rate (Type II error) in a biometric system. It is an important measurement in determining the system's accuracy.

**420. Answer: B**

**Explanation:** A race condition occurs when two or more processes use a shared resource, and the sequence of steps within the software can be executed in an improper order, potentially leading to unexpected and undesirable outcomes.

**421. Answer: C**

**Explanation:** Strong authentication, also known as Multi-Factor Authentication (MFA), involves using two or more of the three authentication methods to verify a user's identity, thereby providing a higher security level.

**422. Answer: B**

**Explanation:** Uniqueness in digital identities ensures that each user is assigned a specific identifier that is distinct from others, which is necessary to track individual actions for accountability.

**423. Answer: C**

**Explanation:** Logical access control refers to the software-based technical tools and components that enforce access control measures for systems, programs, processes, and information, ensuring that only authorized individuals can access and use network resources.

**424. Answer: B**

**Explanation:** IDaaS is a type of Software as a Service (SaaS) offering that typically includes single sign-on (SSO), federated identity management (IdM), and password management services. Primarily designed for managing identities in cloud and web-centric systems, it can also extend to legacy platforms within an enterprise network.

**425. Answer: B**

**Explanation:** An on-premise IdM system is one where all necessary resources, including hardware, software, and licenses, are under the direct physical control of the enterprise. The enterprise uses its team to build, integrate, and maintain the system.

**426. Answer: B**

**Explanation:** A significant issue with IDaaS in regulated industries is the potential inability to remain compliant, as critical identity management (IdM) functions are outsourced, and the service provider may not meet all regulatory requirements.

**427. Answer: C**

**Explanation:** An on-premise IdM solution is most appropriate for managing identities for systems that are not directly connected to the internet, such as networks of certain critical infrastructure and military organizations or networks that are air-gapped for security.

**428. Answer: B**

**Explanation:** Gartner forecasted that starting in 2021, most new system acquisitions would adopt Identity-as-a-service (IDaaS) solutions.

**429. Answer: C**

**Explanation:** A crucial aspect of setting up connectivity in identity management services is guaranteeing secure communication between the components involved.

### 430. Answer: A

**Explanation:** Certificate Authorities (CAs) may not be trusted by default by all the nodes, particularly if an enterprise has implemented its own CA internally and is deploying an outsourced service.

### 431. Answer: B

**Explanation:** The recommended approach for testing the integration of identity services is to test incrementally, starting with test accounts (i.e., not real users), then one department or division as a test case, and finally, the entire organization.

### 432. Answer: C

**Explanation:** It is crucial to integrate federated systems carefully because their dependencies may be complex and intertwined with external organizations and systems, creating compatibility challenges when integration is attempted.

### 433. Answer: C

**Explanation:** A session key is a single-use symmetric key that is used to encrypt messages between two users during a communication session. It is generated anew for each session to enhance security.

### 434. Answer: C

**Explanation:** Discretionary Access Control (DAC) is characterized by the resource owner having the discretion to specify which subjects can access certain resources. This model allows owners to control access based on the authorization granted to users.

### 435. Answer: D

**Explanation:** Mandatory Access Control (MAC) is a security model in which the operating system imposes stringent access control policies, restricting users' ability to install software or modify permissions. It is prevalent in environments requiring robust protection for highly sensitive or classified data. Under MAC, access decisions are determined by system administrators or predefined security policies, ensuring strict control over resource access and minimizing the risk of unauthorized actions.

**436. Answer: C**

**Explanation:** Role-Based Access Control (RBAC) is a model where access to resources is based on the role a user holds within an organization. This model simplifies access control administration by managing permissions according to the operations and tasks associated with a user's job role.

**437. Answer: B**

**Explanation:** Discretionary Access Control (DAC) grants or denies access based on the identity of the subject, such as user identity or group membership. In contrast, Rule-Based Access Control (RBAC) employs specific rules that dictate what can and cannot occur between subjects and objects, and it is not necessarily based on identity.

**438. Answer: C**

**Explanation:** SE Linux, developed by the National Security Agency (NSA, is an example of a system that operates under Mandatory Access Control (MAC) This system enforces strict access control and is designed to protect highly classified data.

**439. Answer: B**

**Explanation:** Hierarchical RBAC allows for role hierarchies, which means roles can inherit permissions and access rights from other roles. This model maps closely to a company's organizational structures and functional delineations, reflecting the hierarchy of authority and responsibility.

**440. Answer: A**

**Explanation:** Stream ciphers are advantageous over block ciphers when streaming communication data, such as in real-time applications like VoIP or multimedia, needs to be encrypted. They can encrypt and decrypt more quickly and scale better with increased bandwidth requirements.

**441. Answer: B**

**Explanation:** The 'Need-to-Know' rule applies to the Mandatory Access Control (MAC) model, where access decisions are not only based on security clearances but also on whether the subject needs to know the information classified at a certain level.

### 442. Answer: C

**Explanation:** Sensitivity labels, also known as security labels, are used in Mandatory Access Control (MAC) Systems contain classifications and categories. These labels enforce access control by determining if a subject's clearance and need-to-know match the classification and category of the object.

### 443. Answer: D

**Explanation:** Attribute-Based Access Control (ABAC) provides the most granularity by using attributes associated with subjects, objects, actions, or contexts to define access policies. This allows for very specific and detailed access control that can consider a wide range of factors.

### 444. Answer: B

**Explanation:** The primary function of constrained user interfaces is to restrict users' access abilities by not allowing them to request certain functions or information or to have access to specific system resources. This is done by providing limited options on menus, restricting database views, or physically constraining the interface, such as an ATM keypad.

### 445. Answer: C

**Explanation:** TACACS+ uses TCP as its transport protocol, which provides a reliable connection-oriented service. RADIUS uses UDP, which is a connectionless protocol and does not guarantee the delivery of packets.

### 446. Answer: A

**Explanation:** 'AAA' stands for authentication, authorization, and auditing. It is sometimes referred to as authentication, authorization, and accounting, but both terms describe the same functionalities of verifying user credentials, granting permissions, and tracking user activity.

### 447. Answer: B

**Explanation:** The major difference between Access Control Lists (ACLs) and capability tables is that ACLs are bound to the object, specifying which subjects have access to it, whereas capability tables are bound to the subject, specifying which objects the subject has access to and the operations allowed.

**448. Answer: B**

**Explanation:** TACACS+ uses a true AAA architecture that separates authentication, authorization, and accounting, which gives network administrators more flexibility in how remote users are authenticated. RADIUS, on the other hand, combines authentication and authorization functionalities.

**449. Answer: C**

**Explanation:** Diameter protocol is designed to provide an upgrade path from RADIUS, with more flexibility and capabilities to meet the new demands of today's complex and diverse networks. It is an AAA protocol that builds upon the functionality of RADIUS to overcome many of its limitations.

**450. Answer: C**

**Explanation:** Context-dependent access control makes access decisions based on the context of a collection of information rather than on the sensitivity of the data. It reviews the situation and decides the appropriateness of access, such as a stateful firewall, making decisions based on packet sequences.

**451. Answer: C**

**Explanation:** In an access control matrix, a capability corresponds to a row outlining what operations a particular subject can perform on various objects. Conversely, an ACL corresponds to a column listing the subjects that have access to a specific object and the level of access they are granted.

**452. Answer: C**

**Explanation:** Diameter is described as a peer-based protocol that allows either end to initiate communication, which is a capability not offered by client/server protocols like RADIUS and TACACS+. This functionality allows the Diameter server to request additional authentication credentials from the user if needed.

## 453. Answer: B

**Explanation:** Mobile IP technology allows a user to move from one network to another while maintaining the use of the same IP address. It provides a home IP address and a care-of address, with the latter changing as the user moves between networks while traffic is forwarded to the current care-of address.

## 454. Answer: B

**Explanation:** The primary purpose of user access reviews is to ensure that there are no active accounts that are no longer necessary. These reviews are conducted periodically, such as every six months, or may be triggered by specific administrative actions to confirm if the accounts still serve a purpose and adhere to the organization's security policies.

## 455. Answer: B

**Explanation:** The provisioning process for a user's digital identity involves reviews and approvals from human resources (HR) staff, the individual's supervisor, and the IT department to ensure that digital identities are issued to the correct individuals.

## 456. Answer: C

**Explanation:** Provisioning typically happens when a new user or system is added to an organization. It is a part of the onboarding process, establishing the user's or system's digital identity within the organization's network.

## 457. Answer: B

**Explanation:** A potential challenge with de-provisioning accounts is that it could leave orphaned resources, such as files or data, that are no longer accessible because the account that owned them has been removed. This can be wasteful and hinder business if the files are needed later on.

## 458. Answer: C

**Explanation:** Documenting the reason for provisioning an account is important because it helps in determining whether the account should remain active or be deprovisioned in the future. This is crucial as rationales for account creation may be forgotten over time, particularly with staffing changes.

**459. Answer: B**

**Explanation:** When an employee is terminated, their user account is usually deprovisioned as part of the termination procedures. This is to ensure that the ex-employee no longer has access to the organization's resources and systems.

**460. Answer: C**

**Explanation:** Periodic system account access reviews are necessary to ensure that there are no unnecessary or potentially privileged system accounts that remain active. These accounts can be forgotten since they are not interacted with directly, yet they may pose a security risk.

**461. Answer: C**

**Explanation:** Human Resources (HR) is not typically involved in system account access reviews, as these reviews pertain to system accounts, which are associated with services and automated agents rather than individual employees.

**462. Answer: B**

**Explanation:** A user access review can be triggered outside of the regular schedule by certain administrative actions such as an extended leave of absence, hospitalization, long-term disability, investigation for possible wrongdoing, or an unexpected disappearance.

**463. Answer: B**

**Explanation:** When de-provisioning a user's account, transferring ownership of the user's resources to someone else is important to prevent operational hindrance. This ensures that important files or data remain accessible and that the business can continue without disruption.

**464. Answer: A**

**Explanation:** Access control consists of administrative controls, which include policies and procedures; technical (or logical) controls, which include system access and network architecture; and physical controls, which include perimeter security and work area separation.

### 465. Answer: C

**Explanation:** Security awareness training falls under administrative controls, which deal with the policies and procedures, personnel controls, supervisory structure, and testing to ensure all security measures align with the company's goals.

### 466. Answer: C

**Explanation:** Physical controls are designed to physically secure the environment and work in conjunction with administrative and technical controls to provide a comprehensive access control system.

### 467. Answer: B

**Explanation:** Personnel controls dictate how employees are expected to interact with security mechanisms and address noncompliance issues. They include procedures for hiring, termination, and access restrictions to prevent unauthorized actions such as deleting financial statements.

### 468. Answer: A

**Explanation:** Network segregation, which can be both physical and logical, controls how different sections of a network communicate with each other, thereby managing the flow of data between segments.

### 469. Answer: C

**Explanation:** Technical controls are security measures that regulate logical access to systems and information, ensuring confidentiality, integrity, and availability of resources.

### 470. Answer: C

**Explanation:** Segregating a company's network into different zones allows for the application of suitable access controls depending on the criticality of devices and the sensitivity of the data processed in each zone.

### 471. Answer: B

**Explanation:** The hybrid approach that uses symmetric and asymmetric encryption methods is often called a digital envelope. This method uses the speed of symmetric encryption for the message and the secure key distribution of asymmetric encryption for the symmetric key.

**472. Answer: B**

**Explanation:** A supervisory structure is an administrative control where each employee has a superior responsible for their actions, linking accountability directly to the management hierarchy.

**473. Answer: C**

**Explanation:** Asymmetric cryptography provides authentication by using a pair of keys (public and private). A message encrypted with an individual's private key can only be decrypted with the corresponding public key, thus authenticating the sender.

**474. Answer: C**

**Explanation:** The importance of maintaining security at a high level by performing regular tasks as part of good access control practices. These tasks are crucial to prevent vulnerabilities and keep the environment secure.

**475. Answer: C**

**Explanation:** Limiting and monitoring the usage of administrator accounts, not increasing them. Redundancy in this context could lead to increased security risks.

**476. Answer: B**

**Explanation:** Object reuse refers to the practice of reassigning to a subject media (like hard drives or USB drives) that previously contained one or more objects, which could potentially include sensitive information.

**477. Answer: B**

**Explanation:** To safeguard against unauthorized disclosure of sensitive information, it's crucial to erase or degauss media containing confidential data before reusing it.

**478. Answer: C**

**Explanation:** TEMPEST technology is designed to suppress spurious electrical signals emitted by electrical equipment, preventing the leakage of sensitive information through such emissions.

**479. Answer: C**

**Explanation:** TEMPEST technology is complex and expensive, and therefore, it is used primarily in highly sensitive areas, such as military institutions, where the highest level of protection against electronic eavesdropping is necessary.

**480. Answer: B**

**Explanation:** White noise is a spectrum of random electrical signals that are used to prevent intruders from distinguishing real information from random noise, thereby protecting against electronic eavesdropping.

**481. Answer: B**

**Explanation:** A control zone utilizes materials in the walls of a facility to contain electrical signals, acting like a large Faraday cage, which prevents unauthorized access to data through electrical signal interception.

**482. Answer: C**

**Explanation:** The Digital Signature Algorithm (DSA) is an example of an asymmetric key algorithm, which involves the use of a pair of keys (public and private keys) that are mathematically related.

**483. Answer: C**

**Explanation:** If media that holds sensitive information cannot be purged of its data, steps should be taken to properly destroy it so that no one else can obtain the information.

**484. Answer: B**

**Explanation:** The main disadvantage of symmetric cryptography with many users is the difficulty in managing a large number of keys, as each pair of users requires a unique key for secure communication.

**485. Answer: B**

**Explanation:** NIDS uses sensors, often placed in promiscuous mode, to monitor network traffic and analyze it for signs of intrusion.

### 486. Answer: D

**Explanation:** An IDS generally consists of sensors, analyzers, and administrator interfaces. Encryption algorithms are used for securing data, not for the detection of intrusions.

### 487. Answer: C

**Explanation:** Signature-based IDSs can only recognize attacks that have been previously identified and have signatures written for them. Zero-day attacks are new and do not have signatures yet, making them undetectable by signature-based IDSs.

### 488. Answer: A

**Explanation:** A HIDS is used to monitor the activities within a particular computer system, such as individual workstations and servers, and is not designed to monitor network traffic or electrical emissions.

### 489. Answer: C

**Explanation:** A statistical anomaly-based IDS operates by creating a profile of the environment's regular activities and then comparing new activities to this profile to identify anything that doesn't match, which could indicate a new attack.

### 490. Answer: B

**Explanation:** Heuristic refers to the IDS's ability to gather different "clues" from the network or system and calculate the probability that an attack is taking place based on those clues.

### 491. Answer: B

**Explanation:** The number of symmetric keys needed for secure communication between n people is calculated using the formula $N(N-1)/2$. For 10 people: $10(10-1)/2 = 45$ keys.

### 492. Answer: B

**Explanation:** When a NIC is put into promiscuous mode, it captures all traffic on the network segment it is attached to, not just the traffic addressed to the host system.

### 493. Answer: C

**Explanation:** In a switched environment, data is transferred through virtual circuits not accessible to a standard IDS sensor. By mirroring traffic to a spanning port, the sensor can analyze traffic from all circuits on the network.

### 494. Answer: C

**Explanation:** Cryptography is intended to store and transmit data in a form that is unreadable to unauthorized users but can be processed and read by those it is intended for.

### 495. Answer: C

**Explanation:** Hieroglyphics were used in ancient Egypt primarily for decorative purposes, to make the life stories on tombs appear more noble and ceremonial.

### 496. Answer: C

**Explanation:** The Atbash encryption method involves flipping the alphabet so that each letter is mapped to a different letter in the flipped alphabet, making it a monoalphabetic substitution cipher.

### 497. Answer: C

**Explanation:** Julius Caesar is known for creating a simple method of encryption by shifting the letters of the alphabet by three positions, known as the Caesar cipher, which is a type of monoalphabetic substitution cipher.

### 498. Answer: B

**Explanation:** ROT13 was used to encode potentially offensive material in online forums, so only those who wished to read it would apply the shift-13 method to decrypt the text.

### 499. Answer: C

**Explanation:** Blaise de Vigenère created a polyalphabetic substitution cipher for Henry III, which used a Vigenère table to facilitate the process and raised the difficulty of encryption and decryption.

### 500. Answer: D

**Explanation:** During World War II, rotor cipher machines were a breakthrough in military cryptography, providing complexity that was challenging to break at the time.

**501. Answer: B**

**Explanation:** William Frederick Friedman is called the "Father of Modern Cryptography" and made significant contributions to cryptanalysis during World War II.

**502. Answer: B**

**Explanation:** DES was based on the Lucifer project at IBM, which incorporated complex mathematical equations and functions that were later adopted and modified by the NSA.

**503. Answer: B**

**Explanation:** Cryptanalysis refers to the study of decrypting encrypted data, utilized by both security experts to enhance cryptographic techniques and by malicious actors to illicitly access information.

**504. Answer: D**

**Explanation:** The sophisticated mathematics used in today's symmetric algorithms is designed to be complex enough to thwart simplistic frequency-analysis attacks, enhancing the security of the encrypted messages.

**505. Answer: A**

**Explanation:** A cryptosystem encompasses the necessary components for encryption and decryption to take place, which include software, protocols, algorithms, and keys.

**506. Answer: A**

**Explanation:** Kerckhoffs' Principle, proposed by Auguste Kerckhoffs in 1883, states that the only secrecy involved with a cryptography system should be the key, and the algorithm itself should be publicly known.

**507. Answer: C**

**Explanation:** A large keyspace in an encryption algorithm allows for more possible key values, which makes it more difficult for an intruder to guess the correct key and decipher the protected information.

**508. Answer: C**

**Explanation:** A one-time pad is an encryption scheme that is deemed unbreakable when implemented properly because it uses a key made up of truly random values that are as long as the message and only used once.

## 509. Answer: C

**Explanation:** For a one-time pad to be considered unbreakable, it must be made up of truly random values, used only one time, and be at least as long as the message.

## 510. Answer: C

**Explanation:** In symmetric encryption, the algorithm remains unchanged, providing a consistent method for encrypting and decrypting data.

## 511. Answer: A

**Explanation:** A running key cipher uses a key that might consist of a book page, line number, and column count, where the sender and receiver have agreed upon a set of books to use as part of the encryption process.

## 512. Answer: B

**Explanation:** The least significant bit (LSB) method in steganography involves altering the least important bits in a file, such as a digital image or audio file, to hide secret data without noticeable distortion or file size changes.

## 513. Answer: C

**Explanation:** Subkeys are keys that are derived from a master key. Different subkeys are used to ensure that the same key is not used over and over again, which would increase security risks.

## 514. Answer: B

**Explanation:** Symmetric encryption algorithms use a combination of substitution ciphers, which replace bits or characters with different ones, and transposition ciphers, which rearrange the bits or characters to hide the original meaning.

## 515. Answer: B

**Explanation:** A substitution cipher uses a key to dictate the substitution process. For example, in the Caesar cipher, the key is the instruction to shift letters up by three places in the alphabet.

**516. Answer: A**

**Explanation:** In the Caesar cipher with a key that instructs a shift of three places, the letter 'm' would be replaced by 'p' since it's three places beyond 'm' in the English alphabet.

**517. Answer: B**

**Explanation:** In a transposition cipher, the key determines the new positions of the values, effectively scrambling the order to hide the original message.

**518. Answer: B**

**Explanation:** Using different keys adds randomness and secrecy, making it more difficult for eavesdroppers to reverse-engineer the encryption process.

**519. Answer: C**

**Explanation:** Simple substitution and transposition ciphers can be vulnerable to frequency-analysis attacks because some letters or patterns are more common in languages, allowing attackers to guess parts of the message.

**520. Answer: B**

**Explanation:** KDFs are used to generate keys with random values, which increases the security of the cryptosystem by ensuring that different subjects have different symmetric keys.

**521. Answer: B**

**Explanation:** The principle of least privilege ensures that users have the minimum level of access necessary to perform their job functions, reducing the risk of unauthorized access or actions.

**522. Answer: B**

**Explanation:** Data classification involves categorizing data based on its value and sensitivity, which helps in applying appropriate security controls to protect it.

**523. Answer: C**

**Explanation:** RBAC assigns permissions to users based on their roles within the organization, simplifying access management and ensuring that users have appropriate access levels.

**524. Answer: D**

**Explanation:** S/MIME (Secure/Multipurpose Internet Mail Extensions) is a protocol used to secure email communications by providing encryption and digital signatures.

**525. Answer: B**

**Explanation:** SSO enables users to authenticate once and gain access to multiple applications or systems without needing to log in separately for each one.

**526. Answer: B**

**Explanation:** Penetration testing simulates attacks to identify and exploit vulnerabilities in a system, helping to assess the system's security posture.

**527. Answer: B**

**Explanation:** Incident response focuses on managing and mitigating the impact of security incidents to restore normal operations and reduce damage.

**528. Answer: C**

**Explanation:** Code review involves reviewing the source code of an application to identify and fix security vulnerabilities before deployment, enhancing software security.

**529. Answer: C**

**Explanation:** Confidentiality ensures that information is accessible only to authorized individuals or systems, protecting it from unauthorized disclosure.

**530. Answer: B**

**Explanation:** HIPAA mandates safeguards to protect the privacy and security of PHI, ensuring that healthcare organizations handle sensitive patient information securely and confidentially.

### 531. Answer: B

**Explanation:** Quantitative risk assessment uses statistical methods and data to quantify risks in terms of monetary value, likelihood, and impact.

### 532. Answer: B

**Explanation:** Hardware Asset Management (HAM) systems are used to track and manage physical assets, such as servers and networking equipment, throughout their lifecycle.

### 533. Answer: A

**Explanation:** RSA (Rivest-Shamir-Adleman) algorithm is a widely used asymmetric cryptographic algorithm for both encryption and digital signatures.

### 534. Answer: C

**Explanation:** SSH (Secure Shell) operates at the Application Layer and provides secure remote login and file transfer capabilities over an unsecured network.

### 535. Answer: C

**Explanation:** Biometric authentication factors, such as fingerprint or iris scans, are considered the strongest because they are unique to each individual.

### 536. Answer: B

**Explanation:** Dynamic Application Security Testing (DAST) simulates attacks against an application in real-time to identify vulnerabilities that attackers may exploit.

### 537. Answer: C

**Explanation:** Chain of custody procedures ensure that evidence collected during incident response is properly documented, handled, and preserved to maintain its integrity and admissibility.

**538. Answer: B**

**Explanation:** Agile methodology emphasizes collaboration, iterative development, and rapid responses to change, making it suitable for software projects requiring flexibility and frequent updates.

**539. Answer: A**

**Explanation:** Integrity ensures that data remains accurate, complete, and unmodified during storage, processing, or transmission.

**540. Answer: C**

**Explanation:** GDPR is a regulation that protects the personal data and privacy of individuals within the European Union (EU) and European Economic Area (EEA), requiring organizations to implement measures to safeguard personal data.

**541. Answer: B**

**Explanation:** BIA evaluates risks based on their potential impact on an organization's critical operations and objectives, helping prioritize risk management efforts.

**542. Answer: C**

**Explanation:** A software license management system helps organizations optimize software license usage, ensuring compliance with vendor agreements and minimizing costs.

**543. Answer: A**

**Explanation:** Diffie-Hellman is a key exchange protocol used to securely negotiate and exchange cryptographic keys over an insecure communication channel.

**544. Answer: A**

**Explanation:** TLS provides secure communication over the web by encrypting data, and ensuring confidentiality, integrity, and authentication of web traffic.

**545. Answer: D**

**Explanation:** Federated identity management systems enable organizations to establish trust relationships and enable seamless access to shared resources across different domains.

**546. Answer: B**

**Explanation:** SAST analyzes an application's source code to identify security vulnerabilities and weaknesses without executing the code, helping developers find and fix issues early in the development lifecycle.

**547. Answer: B**

**Explanation:** A backup and recovery plan outlines procedures for backing up critical data and systems and restoring them after a disruptive event to ensure business continuity.

**548. Answer: C**

**Explanation:** The DevOps model emphasizes collaboration between development and operations teams, automated testing, and continuous delivery to accelerate software development and deployment.

**549. Answer: B**

**Explanation**: Non-repudiation ensures that actions or events cannot be denied or refuted by the parties involved, providing evidence of authenticity and accountability.

**550. Answer: A**

**Explanation:** GLBA requires financial institutions to implement security measures to protect customer information, ensuring the confidentiality and integrity of financial transactions.

**551. Answer: C**

**Explanation:** A risk appetite statement defines an organization's approach to risk-taking and guides decision-making in security governance frameworks.

**552. Answer: B**

**Explanation:** Compartmentalization in information classification refers to organizing information into distinct categories or groups based on sensitivity levels.

**553. Answer: C**

**Explanation:** The Bell-LaPadula model is a security model that enforces strict access control based on hierarchical clearance levels to prevent unauthorized information flow.

**554. Answer: B**

**Explanation:** NIDS monitors network traffic for suspicious activities and alerts security teams to potential threats in real-time.

**555. Answer: B**

**Explanation:** ABAC dynamically adjusts user access based on attributes such as roles, responsibilities, and environmental conditions, providing flexible access control.

**556. Answer: C**

**Explanation:** Black-box penetration testing simulates real-world attacks to assess the effectiveness of security controls and identify vulnerabilities in a system.

**557. Answer: C**

**Explanation:** MTTR measures the average time taken to respond to security incidents, indicating the efficiency of incident response processes and teams.

**558. Answer: A**

**Explanation:** Fuzz testing involves sending random or malformed data inputs to an application to trigger unexpected behavior and identify vulnerabilities.

**559. Answer: B**

**Explanation:** Availability ensures that information and resources are accessible to authorized users when needed, minimizing downtime and disruptions.

**560. Answer: C**

# Answers

**Explanation:** GDPR mandates organizations to protect personal data processed within the EU, regardless of where the processing takes place, ensuring privacy and data protection.

## About Our Products

Other products from VERSAtile Reads are:

 Elevate Your Leadership: The 10 Must-Have Skills

 Elevate Your Leadership: 8 Effective Communication Skills

 Elevate Your Leadership: 10 Leadership Styles for Every Situation

 300+ PMP Practice Questions Aligned with PMBOK 7, Agile Methods, and Key Process Groups – 2024

 Exam-Cram Essentials Last-Minute Guide to Ace the PMP Exam - Your Express Guide featuring PMBOK® Guide

 Career Mastery Blueprint - Strategies for Success in Work and Business

 Memory Magic: Unraveling the Secret of Mind Mastery

 The Success Equation Psychological Foundations For Accomplishment

 Fairy Dust Chronicles – The Short and Sweet of Wonder

 B2B Breakthrough – Proven Strategies from Real-World Case Studies

**VERSAtile Reads**

 CISA Fast Track Master: CISA Essentials for Exam Success

 CISM Fast Track Master: CISM Essentials for Exam Success

 CCSP Fast Track Master: CCSP Essentials for Exam Success

 CLF-C02: AWS Certified Cloud Practitioner: Fast Track to Exam Success

 ITIL 4 Foundation Essentials: Fast Track to Exam Success

 CCNP Security Essentials: Fast Track to Exam Success

 Certified SCRUM Master Exam Cram Essentials

 Six Sigma Green Belt Exam Cram: Essentials for Exam Success

 Microsoft 365 Fundamentals: Fast Track to Exam Success